Life

in the

Labyrinth

**The Labyrinth Trilogy
Book II**

Life
in the
Labyrinth

WRITTEN AND ILLUSTRATED BY

E. J. GOLD

GATEWAYS/IDHHB, INC.
PUBLISHERS

Frontispiece photo by Willem DeGroot

Published by:
IDHHB, INC.
PO Box 370
Nevada City, CA 95959

ISBN: 0-89556-048-8
Library of Congress Card Catalog Number: 86-82759

E.J. GOLD, *CITY IN THE SKY,* OIL ON CANVAS, 36'' x 48'', 1986.

INTRODUCTION

About five years ago, I began expressing with more and more urgency a feeling of dissatisfaction which was becoming progressively acute and which habitually elicited fear and ridicule from my rather close circle of friends.

Most recently I spent the better part of a year working with Mr. Gold on the organization and expansion of this manuscript, trying to penetrate the labyrinth, to expand my understanding and perception from all possible directions.

Now, when I look back at the nebulous quality of my former life among the primates, it all becomes so clear. What I so painfully tried to express was the feeling described here, of being utterly lost in a maze, desperately seeking guidance.

In spite of the fact that my career as a museum designer — one of my most recent projects had been the Strange, Strange World Pavilion at Expo — was proceeding at an excellent pace, that I lacked nothing outwardly and had an extremely generous income, that I was stable emotionally, that I had friends and lovers with whom deep, loving and full relationships had developed, a profound and unshakable conviction remained that I was getting nowhere in life, that I still had no clear idea how I was to move from my present situation and state to where I really wanted to be and knew I could be if I could only discover the means—I already knew that I had the will, the driving force, which had been with me since early childhood—though by all social standards—even of the highest aesthetic—I seemed to be in the best of all possible situations.

I was not particularly caught up in primate pursuits and had already surpassed many normal primate goals such as owning an automobile or a house. My attention was even now firmly fixed toward a spiritual quest.

I had learned long ago that life was not meant to be lived outwardly, but I didn't know how to work with what I had, and where I was. I felt that, although my life seemed to be proceeding in a firm, strong straight line toward ordinary success, I had actually been wandering in aimless circles.

Progressively, I became well-versed in Work ideas and was striving inwardly to prepare myself for entry into a school, although I was rather pessimistic about the likelihood of ever finding one and being allowed to penetrate it. I felt unworthy even though it was what I most desired out of life.

I was well educated and had constant access to lofty ideas at least as they were known in Eastern and Western thought; my whole life was immersed in the ocean of philosophy.

My friends were mostly intellectuals and artists, many of them considered by society in general and the esoteric philosophical community in specific, to be inspired creators and thinkers to whom many others could safely turn for guidance, but when I turned to them I was always disappointed with their conservatism and scholarly atavism which most puzzled me; I could literally watch someone's anxiety grow as I spoke about the emptiness and darkness in which I lived, my words resonating almost violently within those who heard me speak in this way. They seemed utterly terrified, but I had to dare express the horrifying subjective truth of my situation.

I did not have a solid conceptual grasp of my experience; but I was willing to live with it, eschewing didactic obfuscations. Not possessing labyrinth terminology,

I spoke instead of moving between glimpses of "light" which I so wished to remain in forever, and shadows of "darkness" in which I felt myself hopelessly wandering most of the time. It was very painful not to be able to fully grasp something of which I was intuitively aware.

The feeling of darkness and blindness had appeared at regular intervals in my life throughout most of my adult years. Every time it emerged, I attempted to describe it to my friends, but their own emptiness just reflected my own.

I usually ended up feeling more alone, isolated, and despairing than ever. Yet I knew that I was not fabricating something out of psychological instability or mental deviation. I did not suffer from a perversity of the mind which led me into bizarre perceptions. I was healthy and, outside of this one area, considered intelligent and insightful; in fact, many people turned to me for clarity and understanding. The blind leading the blind . . . .

It takes a long time to develop vision, but with proper training and a solid conceptual framework one can learn to see in new categories. It is my hope that this book can provide some of the tools which I have found useful in obtaining a beginning grasp of the labyrinth, that you may benefit from the truth—which leaves me not at peace, as I had imagined, but in even greater turmoil—which I have at last found.

Linda Corriveau
Editor

AUTHOR'S FOREWORD

A SERIOUS WARNING TO THE READER

Should we put references in the text to see appendix? If this were a university text, I might consider it; a course of abstract study and abstract interest... but this book is for serious voyagers, those who really do intend to use these ideas, who aren't going to read a paragraph or two, nod thoughtfully, wander off to some coffeehouse and tear it apart along with Kant and Hegel for a few hours, then wander back home in time for the late night movie.

Further, I don't consider it my responsibility to rectify the failures of whatever education system you might have had the misfortune to endure in your formative years as a young, upcoming primate.

Having spent two miserable semesters teaching remedial third grade elementary level English to adult university students who should have been exploring the mysteries of Beowulf in the original text, singing the Song of Roland, softly chanting the Canterbury Tales, arguing first folio and second quarto alterations in Hamlet and following the intricacies of Philip Jose Farmer, Ezra Pound and Dorothy Parker, I feel that I've more than paid my debt to society, and you're welcome to it.

I am by laws much higher than any primate law, constrained to introduce these ideas to those who come to me in genuine necessity, but nothing in the rule-book says it has to be spoon-fed in monosyllabic, monocultural and monotonous truck-driver language ... so it isn't.

In studying these ideas as presented here, you would be wise to be armed with a dictionary and a healthy education, although nothing in this material is beyond second-year college level English, and the few literary, mythological and philosophical referents—which were intentionally kept to a minimum except where necessary to the sense, germane to the concept or alexipharmic to the destruction of an elegant pun—are well within the grasp of the average high school graduate. If they aren't, perhaps you ought to consider returning to the high school from whence you came, and registering a complaint or enrolling in a night course, whichever seems most *a propos* ... that's borrowed French for copacetic.

Admittedly, this text is a formidable prospect for those with an unsure grasp of the English language, for who the idea of a athalete with a perculator whose on his way irregardless to a realitor because he want's to avoid nucular conflict is a whole nother thing.

If you found the previous paragraph disturbing, this book is probably for you; if it looked all right, maybe you should consider curling up with a good Harlequin novel ... if one can be found.

TABLE OF CONTENTS

Unknowingly we voyage in a labyrinth, a macrodimensional maze of living electrical force, cloaked by a thick layer of ordinary life. Our most serious obstacle is the uncontrollable urge to convert everything to the familiar, to reduce it all to the level of the primate brain; to reject the living, breathing reality of the totality of all possible attention.

When we awaken a higher learning process, we no longer exhibit confusion and disorientation in the macrodimensions. Through special internal processes which we can learn, we are able to penetrate far beyond the ordinary spectrum, into the macrodimensions, resembling consensus reality in form, but radically different in other ways, perceivable only with long, difficult training of the non-machine attention.

E.J. GOLD, *COSMO STREET HALLWAY,*
PEN & INK WASH, 10''x8'', 1975.

CHAPTER 1

Lost in a Mazement

Unknowingly we voyage in a labyrinth, a macrodimensional maze of living electrical force, cloaked by a thick layer of ordinary life. Our most serious obstacle is the uncontrollable urge to convert everything to the familiar, to reduce it all to the level of the primate brain; to reject the living, breathing reality of the totality of all possible attention.

From previous efforts and understanding, we have established a new relationship between the nonbiological essential self and the human biological machine, and have already demonstrated to our satisfaction that the human machine does indeed provide us with the means of transformation; we clearly see the path which we must take.

Knowing that it is necessary to awaken the machine before we can do anything of objective consequence, we have hopefully achieved some stable results.

By this time, we realize that we are now in need of further instructions to incorporate our present knowledge and take us a step further toward our ultimate aim, the formulation of which may not yet be very exact.

It ought to be obvious that we are only at the very beginning of our path, and we are anxious to take further responsibilities as beings, but before we can take effective steps toward fulfilling these responsibilities, we must first understand just precisely where we are, and what we are, in the general scale of things, and where we stand in relation to the Absolute so we can develop a method of work within this context.

We can now come to understand the essential self in its work-role as eternal voyager, exposed to perils and opportunities, purpose and distraction, fatal attraction and ultimate destruction in the nearly infinite immensity of the labyrinth.

In this quest, we lift our gaze from its firm fixation upon the world of the primate, working from this nonhuman perspective wherever we may discover ourselves to be.

In the first book of the Labyrinth Voyager Series, *The Human Biological Machine as a Transformational Apparatus,* the analogy of a fish tank was invoked to establish an approximate description of the human situation relative to higher dimensions which we will from now on refer to as the macrodimensions.

The animal kingdom will once again be of service, providing us with a point of view that we can easily see, understand, and relate to.

A few minutes of simple observation of a rat in a maze will clearly demonstrate to even the densest scientist that it doesn't know that it's in a maze . . . it's simply aware that it can't get at what it wants and that it doesn't know its way, nor—in the absence of sufficiently compelling motivators— does it much care.

It may also dimly suspect that it can't escape; backwards, forwards, sideways—all apparent possible directions maintain the maddening slavery of the maze.

The trapped rat has no way of knowing the overall shape and configuration, rules and functions of the maze, but it may—under the influence of a sudden, unexpected, and unusual traumatic jolt—become somewhat aware of the fact of its imprisonment, if not of its precise nature.

When it comes to mazes, human primates are every bit as predictable as rats, but without the perceptual and emotional clarity, keen attention and intelligence of their hairier cousins.

A lot can be learned about mazes by experimenting with and testing rats. By altering a maze, for example, but keeping the basic clues the same, we see that the rat will follow old clues rather than the new layout of the maze—but after sufficient rewards of the edible variety, it learns to relearn. When hunger strikes, the inconvenience of synaptic restructuring becomes affordable.

With even the most rudimentary understanding of motivational reprogramming concepts, we can develop for ourselves a series of practical persuasions in user-interactive learning games which encourage intuitive, deductive and inductive reasoning and new learning.

Along these same lines, we may begin to make serious inquiries in the realms of repetitive mazes, alternating mazes, mazes that change suddenly and in unexpected ways in mid-game through interactive variables, relative constants and the absence of objective, or absolute, constants.

We ought to be easily able to make the rather feeble conceptual leap from simple observation of rats encumbered with a fairly primitive intelligence, to ourselves, totally unencumbered by intelligence, bound by artificial limits of memorized educational patterning which functions relative only to a known, oversimplified cultural environment, by which we have learned to apply old responses to cope with new stimuli.

Well, enough philosophy, already; the fact is, both rats and human primates tend to experience essentially the same problems of stress and social pressure, and possess—prior to cultural conditioning and psychoemotional imprinting, which is to say, the usual deep-brain impulse-responsive pain and pleasure formatting—precisely the same initial intuitional innocence largely through the inattention which can only come from lack of self-motivation in the absence of environmental and biological stimuli, and the general perceptual occlusion which results from environmental alienation, a hazy uncaring withdrawal which is symptomatic of deep-seated unexamined fears about things I'd rather not think about just now.

If we are to produce a potent method for our excursions into the macrodimensions, we need only recognize that one rat can be encouraged to venture outward into dark and unknown territory, while another rat cannot bring itself out of its mechanically imposed inertness, no matter what the provocation.

Still, this doesn't actually ensure that anything will come of it; after all, even the most experienced rat is still subject to the maze, still a prisoner, a laboratory animal subject to outside whim, and in this sense—but *only* in this sense—the rat is not free.

Freedom is a subtle and elusive intangible which lies in an unexpected direction, far beyond the bounds of biological slavery and hard-edged walls, as we will soon discover.

Never could understand why—given the same training, the same opportunities, the same and even additional exposure to the maze—nine out of ten rats never seem to be able to extricate themselves from the pleasant robotic muck of animal life.

The labyrinth: a macrodimensional maze camouflaged by the fabric of biological boundaries. In ordinary life, no matter what we do or accomplish, no matter where we go or who we become, we find ourselves ultimately a prisoner of the rigid rut and, submerging ourselves in a nonstop self-invoked bombardment of daily pressures, distractions and self-pity, manage somehow to successfully avoid all real help.

If we know how to look, we can seize the opportunity to work our way through the passages, pitfalls and primrose paths of the macrodimensional maze; but we don't know how to look, and in the beginning we work to fathom the reality that we can be in the maze and yet be completely unaware of it.

Voyagers—which is what we really are—seldom understand or are aware, and can easily fail to recognize the labyrinthine quality of what they are experiencing, because they lack the power of serious, rooted and undistractable attention behind the physical senses with which to view it.

We fail to recognize that we have passed this way many times before, that we have made this or that turn. And, more importantly, *we fail to recognize the futility of everything we have done in the trivial pursuits of primate life.*

But futility is the name of this game; we learn young to flow downstream, toward some awesome, unknowable end, some great, all-engulfing cosmic septic system.

We have thoroughly bought into the cultural norm, perpetuating a pathetically passive posture in relation to the maze—at the same time experiencing all the frustration, anger and fear of any lost, frightened and hungry rat.

Immersed in sleep and stunned by fear, we automatically assume that our house is all in order; that everything is always exactly the same as we expect it to be.

In our preoccupation with trivial distractions of the biological machine, our superficial attention races quickly, almost in embarrassment, past the majestic vistas of macrodimensional events, which we evidently feel compelled to translate immediately or sooner, into the most pedestrian of all possible worlds.

We are neither amused, astonished nor amazed. This translation into the primate is a genuine sickness, as clinical as any commonly accepted medical condition.

Because the essential self with its qualities of attention and presence is able to view things differently, it, on the other hand, is able to perceive crossover into direct maze-perception when it takes place.

Imagine driving a car and, contrary to our customary habit, viewing the car as stationary, the road actually surrounding and being absorbed by the vehicle, more precisely the vehicle's windscreen, sliding past the side windows, spewing itself out the back, after which, it recycles and comes out of a tiny hole in front, expanding and flowing around the car once again.

This is the nature of our whole experience in macrodimensions. We have been trained to compartmentalize our experiences, to isolate their connectors, thus overlooking the subtle continuity amidst apparent change and discontinuity. We have a flip-flop perception of events; where there is change, we see stability; where there is stability, we see change. What we believe is real is definitely illusion, and what we believe is illusion is probably real.

Compulsive primate hallucinations constantly impose an artificial grid of time and space on our purely sensory and mental experience.

We view our passage through Creation from the point of view of an artificially decided upon direction of space and time in direct contradiction to what we already know from geometry, mathematics and physics, periodically updating our perception of events with slight changes in our space-time model, although carefully avoiding the full consequences of what we really know from these disciplines.

I don't mean to complain, but we act as if the primate world really exists, as if we have a direct interface with it, as if there is an absolute certainty and tangible quality to it, when in fact none of it exists—in the sense that we take it to exist—even remotely. We have walled ourselves into a veritable Garden of Familiarity and now we are trapped in it with no hope of escape.

Knowing our propensity for self-illusioning, it isn't at all surprising to find that we have developed a mythology of banishment from the same garden in which we are forced to live out the remainder of our days.

The majority of those voyagers who happen to accidentally find themselves momentarily wandering in the macrodimensions are unaware of the change, and should they somehow become aware of this unaccountable alteration in reality-perception, may end up explaining their experience to someone with a Ph.D. and two hefty orderlies to protect them.

We can always emulate our fellow barely-upright-primates, shuffling aimlessly through the maze oblivious to the subtly clamorous experiences that present themselves to us, or we can awaken to our surroundings and direct ourselves with intelligence and understanding.

Being rather reluctant voyagers, human primates have, through none of their own intention, formed a preconceived idea of the way things should be, and therefore refuse obvious choices; if given the opportunity to follow their natural inclinations, most humans will obey the cultivated rut of brain and body, wherever they may lead.

As popular as it may be, blind, robotic, slavish obedience to habit is considered by the experienced labyrinth voyager a very inelegant method of macrodimensional functioning.

We learn the maze by rote, voyaging in typical human mechanical fashion, and even occasionally arrive accidentally by this method at the heart of the labyrinth, and so long as we remember to do everything exactly the same, and no aberrations of our routine occur, we will seem as if maze-bright, until something happens which isn't exactly on the menu....

Someone really soaked in the wine of primate life, who may have wandered seventy trillion and two times through the same macrodimensional sector will fail to make the Palladian connection; the tendency is to lose contact with the macrodimensional state of consciousness.

Numberless primates have been and seen...yet, through some strange vagary of the mind, blissfully forgotten; many more there are, who didn't see, whose occlusion indicates that they were just plain perceptually inept.

All this can lead any outside observer to conclude that a bizarre form of culturally-induced schizophrenic alienation occurs between maze consciousness and consensus human reality, agreed upon by convention, which in relation to macroconsciousness can hardly be considered to represent consciousness.

**Human primates
Evidently think
They are all alone
In their sector,
And they should be.**

E.J. GOLD, *HOME SWEET HOME,* PASTEL, 30''x 22'', 1987.

CHAPTER 2

Maze Brightness

When we awaken a higher learning process, we no longer exhibit confusion and disorientation in the macrodimensions. Through special internal processes which we can learn, we are able to penetrate far beyond the ordinary spectrum, into the macrodimensions, resembling consensus reality in form, but radically different in other ways, perceivable only with long, difficult training of the non-machine attention.

As a child of thirteen and fourteen, I found my bedroom overrun with lab rats, and more or less as an afterthought—I had no other use for them, not being particularly attracted to vivisection and the like—built a few mazes to study rat behavior.

One item stood out clearly in my observations of dozens of rats stumbling, bumping and sniffing their way toward their final reward as they learned to synthesize experiential data through a primitive form of deduction...or didn't learn, and nearly starved to death.

I discovered, independently of texts on behavioral sciences, something which I later learned was by convention called *maze brightness,* which could be defined for the moment as "becoming able to find new paths through the

maze toward the reward-point through sheer repetition'',
from which we could, if we weren't overly concerned about
how far we could quantum leap, deduce that some rats
eventually become aware of the general rules of maze
construction, of course only on a purely subjective-instinctive
nose-and-gut level.

I discovered through this a special learning process
which could enable the rat to solve not only one known maze
but virtually any maze it may thereafter happen to encounter
by accident or design.

I also concluded, probably rightly, that such a rat
would, eventually—having blundered its way through a
sufficient number of mazes—in spite of itself, begin to dimly
recognize the inescapable fact that it is in a maze and that,
moreover, it cannot—at least by present means—remove
itself to parts unknown.

Once this first all-important recognition has been
achieved, without which nothing further is possible in any
direction except down, it can begin to perceive and analyze
its surroundings as they actually are, and not as its
unexamined fears and perceptual occlusions have caused it
to imagine them to be.

Because the perceptual-emotional conflict will have, for
the moment, been resolved, it will no longer exhibit the
compulsion to maintain a self-constructed veil of confusion
and disorientation.

One would think the thrill of observing that single rat
which, out of dozens, suddenly gave indications of having
become aware of the maze would soon pall, but *au
contraire* ... the shared excitement of this simple yet
magnificent discovery never failed to strike me as anything
less than downright apotheotic, and any behavioral scientist
worth his or her weight in potassium nitrate who says any
different is spouting pure scoria.

A rat achieves maze-brightness, and its eyes seem
somehow at once older and younger; general posture and
behavior toward the environment and toward itself show
radical signs of alteration. It seems less frantic, more self-
assured, and noticeably less self-destructive.

At the same time, one can see visible signs of excitement as a new sense of freedom descends overwhelmingly upon it, the same sense of freedom which humans who have discovered what they call "enlightenment" experience. Of course for humans, this first glimpse of real freedom, not from the maze but from self-induced boundaries, purely psycho-emotional limitations, does not last very long and soon enough, the customary humdrum primate activity reasserts itself.

In the guise of ordinary existence, the maze is all the more diabolical because it has been hidden by itself, yet ultimately, it is the same sprawling macrodimensional complex of corridors and chambers, openings and closings, twistings and turnings reduced to the flat hard-edge walls of organic reality.

Like the complacent rats who fall so easily into apathy—if, indeed, they ever emerge from it—especially after the first glimmerings of rudimentary maze-awareness has presented itself, human primates whose perception had become momentarily open to the whole macrodimensional vision of the unobstructed labyrinth seem to be in an awful hurry to lock themselves into a closet once again.

It might be possible to artificially induce maze awareness and transition into macrodimensional space, but we can fully expect that any resulting momentary understanding which may have been gained will almost instantaneously be mangled, mashed and mauled in the all-devouring jaws of primate convention and found thoroughly indigestible.

At the same time, we are presented with the first real opportunity to penetrate far beyond the ordinary reality spectrum, in a far-seeing and sweeping vision, somewhat resembling consensus reality in form, but radically different in its significance, scale and intensity.

Pure macro-molecular structure becomes visible, matter is revealed as swirling patterns of raw energy, and time becomes nonexistent—a simple expedient to encapsulate an event or to move from one frozen energy-tableau to another; then we know that we are beginning to see things as they really are . . . but we mustn't mention this to anyone in a lab smock if we don't want to spend the rest of our lives interpreting Rorschach blots, calling off Rhine cards and singing *doda kupanga udoda kukala, doda kupanga ukala shatti* background vocals for Leon Russell.

An understanding of what this really means in the objective sense comes only much later when we have demonstrated how even a jungle-wise Zulu can get lost in the bush.

When we have developed total trustworthiness, shown our fortitude and continued enthusiasm in the face of endless repetition, clearly exhibited signs of unshakable loyalty to the Work, successfully separated ourselves from the ways and attitudes of the primate, we will have earned the right to become involved in a different type of work, something beyond the primate.

This "other type of work" can only result from serious and concentrated efforts to enter and perform work obligations in macrodimensional chambers, in unimaginable domains, and to perform such work in ways not at all to the liking of primate directives and biological imperatives of the human biological machine.

Best, then, to be taken everywhere by the hand and shown, but what good is it, if we cannot also at the same time wake up at our own initiative, and survey the very height and breadth of the labyrinth?

Ah, but we must first recognize that there *is* a maze *and that we are in it*. If we haven't achieved at least this one small step, then how can we expect to make the giant leap, to bring ourselves into the waking state, *when it is important to do so?*

Help, real help, is available only to those already well on their way toward nonprimate life, who show an already deeply rooted aptitude for the labyrinth, who have demonstrated themselves to be courageous voyagers, despite personal fears of the more terrifying aspects of the labyrinth, shown the potential ability to perform special work under very difficult and often overwhelming conditions, and most important, do not display the kind of delicate psycho-emotional nature we were likely to see in children who left summer camp the first or second week.

When one considers the profound time limit imposed upon a working school and the small number with whom one can work seriously, it only makes sense that any training effort is concentrated in those who show the highest potential, to isolate the winners and eliminate the losers.

There is, among new voyagers—most of whom never quite make the grade and of whom this is typically symptomatic—a certain amount of impatience to experience unusual, meaning exotic and dangerous, sectors of the maze, but before exposing ourselves, along with our predictably runamuck machines, to the excitement of these deliciously dangerous environs, a number of preparatory steps must be taken to increase our reasonable chances of survival, not for ourselves, but for the sake of the Work, so that our training and transformation is not completely wasted.

Underlying it all must be a strong base of natural ability—*aptitude and attitude*. Only then can any training and acquired—but self-imposed and maintained—discipline have any lasting value.

If we wanted to improve our ability to upscale into the macrodimensions without understanding the purpose of voyaging, we could work from a list of mechanical methods, as can be found in certain popular systems today, where techniques for macrodimensional voyaging are transmitted down the generations with the notable absence of just one little insignificant element: a method for awakening and working in the higher dimensions.

Navigation during active voyaging depends upon a higher learning process, which we call pattern-recognition. Yet recognition is impossible *unless we can see.*

A certain higher intelligence can be acquired in the macrodimensions, but human primate intelligence is all-but-useless, *because it only refers to the life of the human biological machine.* Acquired human intelligence will only blind us to the labyrinth and make us slaves to the boundaries of the primate world.

What is really useful is a method of developing intelligence through active interaction, learning *from* the game how to *play* the game, and in at least one important sense, voyaging is a game, on a very much higher level than we are used to playing; a game in which the stakes are far higher, and correspondingly much more dangerous.

As one would expect from such a game, there are natural limits beyond which primates do not wander, obediently following powerful tribal taboos which have become the custom over the millennia, and no wonder . . . our social usefulness becomes questionable at best once we have begun playing the labyrinth game in deadly earnest.

The Labyrinth Game has been called the Master Game, the Great Game, the Bead Game; only self-motivation, self-initiation, the ability to shake ourselves out of sleep, to make ourselves move from the zero point, to bring ourselves from the immobilized posture of inertness, will produce results in this most dangerous game.

One comes out of inertness, builds acceleration and gathers momentum for macrodimensional voyaging only through sheer repeated effort in voyaging; we become adept at puzzle solutions by working puzzles; one learns to work under stress by working under stress; one learns to work under conditions of profound and incessant distraction by working under conditions of profound and incessant distraction. This is important, because *the maze is composed almost entirely of distractions.*

One can say that its walls, corridors and working chambers are distractions in themselves, distractions which are alternately compellingly attractive or repulsive according to one's present state, which in turn depends upon the degree of influence upon oneself of the primate machine.

Reacting as a primate, one would tend, through sheer gravity of negative emotion and machine habits, to plummet once again into the invitingly seductive occlusion of the human primate domain, topologically speaking.

In the waking state, however, we see clearly that what we had ordinarily taken to be a variety of disconnected events are, in fact, just parts of a single thing which, if we could perceive its totality, would give us a direct experience of the Absolute.

Patterning is a natural part of our perception, but pattern recognition depends entirely upon our ability to eliminate occlusion, to accept larger and larger perceptual-informational topological field structures, not necessarily anthropocentric, taking an entirely different, somewhat less obstructed, view of the morphology and scale of the universe.

In the past, cultures existed which remained in open contact with macrodimensional forces and entities but we who arise from primate civilizations of the Western hemisphere are presently forced to secretly pass down the initiations of shamanism.

Shamanism; a collective name for the categorical study and practice of methods of macrodimensional voyaging. In its highest form it also contains all data necessary to understand work which is to be accomplished through such voyaging.

The shaman was the earliest explorer of the macrodimensions. Long ago, the shaman developed very precise techniques for movement across dimensions and came to understand and transmit to initiates who followed—chronologically, not slavishly—the real significance of visions of what came to be called the Kingdom, at the heart of which is what Western mystics call the Crystal Palace, beneath which lies the secret of the Labyrinth, never given even by oral tradition; it is something to be found only by personal voyaging and discovery. Such knowledge of voyaging and understanding of work in the macrodimensions would be roughly equivalent to graduate work leading to a Doctorate in Labyrinthology in even the most stringent of our ordinary universities.

But there is no Doctorate of Labyrinthology in our universities, although a Medieval university might have issued one; our present, wildly destructive technocratic culture has become so wholly alienated from the living world that it fears any exploration outside the realm of the agro-industrial-military complex, and a possible mass exodus into unknown and economically useless macrodimensions. Such fears are not unusual among robotic government agencies, and have found fertile soil in just about all established cultural powerholders in the whole context of the human history of earth.

If I tell you the meaning,
Your mind
Will follow the meaning;
As attention follows mind,
You won't get the meaning.

E.J. GOLD, *A STRANGE EVENING,* OIL ON CANVAS BOARD,
20'' x 24'', 1987

CHAPTER 3

The Ultimate Puzzle

The labyrinth, as would any maze, has puzzle-like characteristics; obeying the rules of puzzle-solving should, if the laws of the maze are understood and the signs are read correctly, enable us to voyage consciously as well as remember previous passages and have a connected overview which takes into account everything we have ever learned in the maze.

The labyrinth, like any other maze, has puzzle-like characteristics, although it was never intentionally designed as a puzzle. Obeying the rules of puzzle-solving will—if we understand the rules correctly and have read the signs aright, enable us to voyage consciously through the macrodimensions, traversing the labyrinth as easily as we would solve a puzzle.

Computer games would be very useful instruction for labyrinth navigation, to gather puzzle-solving clues and to apply such clues in relation to the real labyrinth.

Personal computers allow us to construct special games, played within user-interactive teaching mazes, where intuitive, deductive and inductive learning skills can become sharpened, and reflex reactions tested.

Playing a game within a self-generating repetitive maze which unaccountably—to the new and unskilled voyager—alters itself law-conformably in the same ways as the macrodimensions seem to alter, can provide a very accurate foundation for the understanding of right action in relation to the labyrinth.

As in the labyrinth, an individual is liable to wander endlessly through the same five, six, seven, eight, or nine different chambers encountering a succession of macro-characters, responding with the same general gamut of acquired reflex reactions which had determined the outcome of the game from its very inception.

Because the game conforms to the same set of mathematical laws which govern the multi-dimensional labyrinth, both lateral and vertical movement through the domains will obey a subset of probability; connectives may or may not be apparent to the voyager; fortunately for the peace of mind of shamen everywhere, the factors which allow movement can be discovered by the attentive voyager only during the course of *intentional* involvement with the game.

The operant logic will not necessarily be obvious to an uninitiated player, but nevertheless it will be consistent with itself within the context of the whole; apparent unrelated-ness, insignificance, and incoherence are indications of misunderstanding and misinterpretation, a perimetric blind spot that renders us unable to see things from the right perspective.

The ability to think in new categories and extend the boundaries of one's presence are the two most important tools we have available; they provide the ability to establish new relationships between objects, events and characters, new patterns of action, and new solutions to problems old and new.

We cannot really say that the labyrinth reflects our games and puzzles; it would be far more correct to say that human primate puzzle games reflect real problems of the maze, that the games we think we invent actually tend to reflect reality, however dimly.

By playing certain kinds of games where clues are assembled in various ways, the quantum leap can be made from the purely mental game which might be presented via computer to a very real game in which a maze is being traversed—the same principles apply.

The maze is not constructed; it is a natural outgrowth of a mathematical formulation of such potency that some of its geometric matrix results in mass-energy density—a tangible universe in which space and time are pure conventions; mass and energy are variables in relation to one another and constants when taken as a whole, the totality of which is subject to complete conversion in a zero-centered balance game.

In the labyrinth, reality is fleeting and intensely subjective. That is why we must first know who we are; only then can we even begin to understand where we are, why we are here, and our possible destinations.

We may now make distinctions between higher and lower dimensions; macrodimensions and microdimensions; upscaling and downscaling; clarity function increase and decrease; perceptual occlusion rise and fall; macrodimensional inhabitants celestial and infernal; angels or demons; we tend to think of macro-beings in terms of rank, gradation, importance, power, orientation toward "good" and "evil", all human aspects which reflect our homocentric view, a universe revolving around earth, the absolute center, and everything, even to the farthest reaches, pointing directly toward us.

Chambers refer to the morphology of any stabilized field anomaly, a frozen tableau, sealed and isolated but connected to passable boundaries with other chambers on both vertical and lateral axes. Chambers relate to voyaging in the sense that we can, with exact knowledge, invoke ourselves directly and predictably into one or another chamber, on a specific macrodimensional level.

Space: a much looser term with a psychological or psychophysical referent—a carry-over from a street jargon developed during the nineteen-sixties by resurging metaphysical labyrinthine voyagers freely breaking contemporary social taboos, and accomplishing little else, through the use of mind-altering substances. It refers to the subjective experience one can have of chambers and dimensions, meaning their qualitative aspect.

Spaces will have smells, textures, depth, weight, thickness, consistency, color, and atmosphere; they will carry moods, emotions, feelings, and sensations of a very definite type. They will also contain data, understanding, cognitions, perceptions and knowledge. They will be familiar or foreign, attractive or repulsive, comfortable or eerie.

We can enter a space, leave a space, sense a space, break a space, space out...the difference is, you'll never hear of a professional voyager chambering out.

The labyrinth; a giant multi-dimensional cardboard cut-out whose inner matrices form along invisible ley lines juxtaposed with alternating topological connections and discontinuities.

As in any elaborate geometric construct, access points and blockages are to be found everywhere. Some blockages actually exist objectively...heat expansion impedance effects in the labyrinth itself...others artificially created by ourselves. Where there is no wall, we painstakingly erect an area of futility to satisfy our own primate sense of security.

In the real world, the unobstructed universe in which our morphological presence has expanded into the whole field of all possible attention-points, we are rarely prepared for unconnected events and rarely, if ever, see things coming—even though we may see clear signals long in advance.

Essential self and machine reactions to the maze are extremely variable. Any voyager is liable to feel lost, incoherent, disoriented, complacent, fearful, panic-stricken, confused or just plain stupid, steeped as we are in that annoyingly dense form of stupidity that seems to arise out of nowhere during periods of machine-threat.

During moments of threat, we can use—if we have the stamina and the instinct to do so—the invocation of presence as a weapon, or, at the very least, as a means of protecting ourselves from various dangers encountered in the course of voyaging through the labyrinth. The invocation of presence, the addition of quanta of attention-energy to the domain defined by our presence-morphology, can also be used as a means of protecting others against negative machine emotions in reflex response to macrodimensional events.

Naturally, this isn't the most desirable use of the invocation of presence and collection of clarity-function in the form of units of ergs; the invocation of presence has a much higher function; we can see it as a surefire method guaranteeing the free passage of the essential self, the nonphenomenal voyager, through ordinarily impassable dimensional and chamber boundaries.

Voyaging in the macrodimensions, we want to be more than just a pair of eyes, ears and a mouthful of hypnagogic prattle; we want to actually be present in these dimensions, to observe the traces of our voyaging profoundly impregnating our being, making permanent creases of understanding in our nonphenomenal brow.

When the collected attention has been intentionally distributed through the chamber, following a natural shaman-oriented priority of chamber-activities, we will find that the primate mind has momentarily ceased its endless repetitious chatter; mechanical mental associations and automatic brain-generated emotions have ceased to put themselves in the way of our seeing.

When we find ourselves somewhere over the rainbow, caught up in the associative processes of the mind, we will find that we lose perspective on what is going on in the chamber.

It is not with the mind that we can grasp the nature of events in the labyrinth. The mind is an obstruction to this process, always one step behind, grasping at rapidly dimming after-images, unconnected to energy flow, just barely catching the reverberations.

Our earliest work efforts were directed toward bringing the machine into the waking state, and developing this rightful rapport between the machine and the essential self, but from now on, we'll be concentrating on the problems of the essential self as a labyrinth voyager, particularly in relation to its shamanic ability to function in macrodimensions.

The labyrinth reveals who we are in a very particular way. It gently coaxes us into unknown lands where we are expected to function at our best, and where we are ruthlessly appraised for our overall shortcomings and aptitudes.

It will happen that every once in a while we will find ourselves feeling stuck in a chamber or a strange morphology, and we'll feel the urge to shapeshift. Spaces open up and we experience vivid changes; objects take on an eerie luminosity; distances seem impossibly stretched, distorted.

But how dare we think we're equipped for a fast lateral shapeshift across the sixth macrodimensional level so long as we remain in our present condition?

Here we bloody well are, out on our morning constitutional, mucking about in areas dark and unknown, depending for our very lives on old, worn out equipment—all those clever little primate tricks we've learned—but it's all useless, even dangerous, in labyrinth domains more appropriate to a wily four-billion-year-old shamanic warrior, but terribly inappropriate for a human primate with the emotional level of a two-year-old child prone to sandbox tantrums at the slightest provocation.

We are connected, roped together, for the duration; an exploration team, each dependent upon the others and, unless we are one of those rare birds, a macrodimensional lone ranger, it is only as a team that we can develop our work.

**Almost anything
Can be used as a key,
If used voluntarily
And consciously
Provided you can find
A lock.**

E.J. GOLD, *INVOCATIONAL CHAMBER #330,*
PEN & INK WASH, 12''x9'', 1975.

CHAPTER 4

The Keys to Elegant Voyaging

The keys to elegant labyrinth voyaging are generally those little, nagging, insignificant items which we would ordinarily dismiss as inconsequential; one such key is the rudder with which we steer ourselves through the labyrinth.

Voyaging depends strongly upon learning to recognize releasing, opening and unlocking and triggering combinations; a combination in this sense can be an object, word, posture, phrase, sound, movement, gesture, even a joke or pun... virtually any mechanism of sound, sight, smell, motion or thought which creates an access point or opening which would otherwise be closed.

Combinations are commonly found in games, mostly puzzle games, and a popular form of this is the computer game; with the right combinations, one can open doors, pass through walls, gain entry or exit, obtain necessary devices and knowledge, or easily execute a lateral transition from one chamber to another using a precision sequence of dance-like movements, hopefully graceful....

Most of the really important keys we'll be using to voyage in the labyrinth are those which are casually dismissed in the primate view as insignificant, trivial, ridiculous, and even humiliating, and of course they go consistently unnoticed . . . except to clowns, stand-up comics, street mimes and other sinister creatures of the night.

Aside from environmentally-prompted keys we might find lying abundantly around, we can also take our clues from inside, suggesting perhaps that we follow instinct, responsive—but not reflexively so—to a wider domain of possible attention-points, a larger dimensional field.

Once we have intuited our clues to passing through the boundaries from chamber to chamber, we may use them, and if they prove to be right combinations, we find ourselves sailing off once again, out the chamber door and through the labyrinth, zig-zagging wildly toward our new destination and, taking advantage of the karmic wind that ordinarily would propel us downward to our just reward, we take care to avoid the doldrums, the bound-in-irons of deadly calm, and cross-tacking to and fro in such a way as to travel the most distance with the greatest possible amount of unnecessary effort, conscious dispersal, ragged confusion, and concentrated amusement, we achieve our lateral transition. That's the easy part. Vertical scaling is a different story altogether.

Every once in a while, it might occur to us to do something slightly eccentric; this could produce lateral transition . . . it could also produce a lot of other things, and isn't recommended for the unschooled voyager.

Attitude, mood, mental set, posture, tempo, time, place and people or a reasonable macrodimensional facsimile—all these factors combined provide the launching pad of probability for dimension-hopping.

We need, most of all, the spirit of risk, adventure, the daring to experiment. Naturally, once in a while, in the spirit of adventure, we might make a little mistake . . . .

In a computer game, a mistake is not serious, at least to the user; it means only that the game is finished; like an actor after a performance, we can quit, walk away and do something else, or we may decide to continue, to restore our position prior to the moment the "tilt" sign lit up; we can choose to begin all over again, or we can trash the disc and send for something easier.

But in the real world, a mistake can be deadly, and in the real world, dead is dead... and once we're dead, there isn't much point in trying to do anything beyond what the dead usually do when they're dead.

If we haven't already gotten ourselves killed or mangled with all our clever macrodimensional bungling, then, when we smell the toast burning, we will intuitively—remembering our previous mistakes—quickly stop everything, check our position, take rapid stock of the situation, sniff the air and, if we detect an odor of sulphur dioxide, methane and ammonia, perhaps take an alternate route or stop eating so much chocolate . . . .

Straightline hotwire associative thought-processing can only serve to hinder us as we respond by well-planned spasmodic reflex to the various traps and traumatic shocks of the labyrinth, but we worry needlessly; it will soon become apparent that there just isn't any way of outguessing the twists and turns that lie ahead of us; fact is, often we'll be mighty hard-pressed to find any discernible difference between the normal significance of an object in the primate sector and its usefulness and function in the macrodimensions, which nine times out of ten will be entirely unrelated, and utterly unfathomable even under extreme pressure to crack its inscrutable silence....

We should not be overly startled to discover that certain objects which in ordinary circumstances are quite valuable, unexpectedly lose their usefulness in the macrodimensions with the possible exception of spectacles, testicles, wallet, cigars....

Remembering what we did three or four games ago, perhaps even in a different game, or three or four lifetimes ago is another important aspect of successful voyaging. No amount of luck will be very useful if we do not remember what we did. Without remembering, we are condemned to repeat our mistakes forever; but this is not the sort of remembering for which we can depend upon the mind or any other function which rightly belongs with—and performs its own one-way swan-song in syncopated duet with—the human biological machine.

For this kind of remembering, we must develop something which survives the death of the machine, something which is called, in our technical language, *understanding*, a semi-intuitional recall, a sixth sense which comes from unprocessed knowledge, that tells us that something is wrong, even if we don't exactly know what.

No ordinary way of approaching life can determine how we are to view things in the labyrinth, what their ultimate utility or function will be, what dangers are set before us; no fixed set of rules will apply to every voyage; the only thing we can predict is that, even when we seem able to guess what tomorrow will bring, the truth is that everything is always totally unpredictable, and it's just the statistical distribution of probability that makes it look as if it isn't.

We must eventually form a somewhat connected overview, realizing that, as Heraclitus once said, and Democritus eloquently repeated, "One cannot step twice into the same river, for the water into which you first stepped has flowed on," meaning that even if the event could be duplicated, it would be happening in a slightly different field, and he was right; nothing will ever be the same twice, and it won't do us any good to compare the present situation with past experience even if we could take into account everything we've ever learned forever . . . .

But with knowledge transubstantiated into understanding, when we do happen to smell something burning, we'll at least be able to discern that this time, it probably isn't the toast . . . .

Certain chambers may appear populated with creatures strange, sinister, and fearsome, encouraging us to just squeak by, missing the chance to fully savor the whole, digging deeper until we understand what we've got hold of. If we escape a trap too quickly, we won't have time to examine the irreparable damage.

Sometimes it can be valuable to relax the machine, but given the fact that certain macrodimensional creatures are very unforgiving—although in a totally impersonal way—and very deadly, we shouldn't depend on it.

We mustn't be afraid to make mistakes, because mistakes are how we learn, generally too late, and to no point because the opportunity is lost.

In the labyrinth, fear will instantly catapult us into the lowest of primate levels, while panic makes us react reflexively, do things we never intended; our judgment becomes distorted; we lose our place, our sense of perspective. When we try, out of a primate-generated sense of pride, a deep, personal fear of humiliation, to cover our panic, we tend to make even worse self-destructive decisions. The cure is generally far worse than the disease.

If we apply it intentionally, voluntarily and knowingly at the exact counterpoint in the general rhythm of an event, panic—as a form of conscious theatre—can definitely be a potent part of right combination; we could dangle a bit of dental floss in a cup of tea, extend pinkie, smile, and say "Mildred, bring cookies", then when the cookies arrive, toss them in the air and in a wild panic, pour the by now quite cool tea in a neat arc over the entire length of the new cream-colored Chinese silk sofa.

All this might sound preposterous, or dangerous if you destroyed two years' budget to buy the sofa, but then, isn't that same fear of extravagant absurdity exactly what keeps clowns working, and confines the greater run of human primates to a neatly boundaried domain a good, healthy distance from the off-limit zones? . . . .

We can't be sure of our results when we suddenly make an improvised move that we suspect will radically alter our course and which we recognize as a desperate—and probably fatal—gamble; what we do in haste may destroy what we have been consciously building for our work.

In every set of domains there is always one common connective which may not be conjunctive or congruent but which gives common ground to all domains, both simple and complex-connected.

It may not be immediately evident, but at some point we will become aware of a kind of central switching exchange, a *Tiphareth,* from which all other domains are only a phone call away. This central exchange can be in itself either passive or active in relation to the shamanic voyager.

If we persevere, we will also come to ferret out that process by which we actually force the distribution of probability our way, offering an ejection point out of the darkness; a bit drastic, perhaps, but we will be seriously considering emergency procedures later, some of them not all that pleasant.

By waiting—and waiting *well* , neither impatiently nor nonchalantly—for the right combination to occur, we can take advantage of the open trunk lines, and climb onto the bus on which we can exit from our present location in the labyrinth, passing inevitably through the central switching station, the heart of the labyrinth.

The labyrinth may change, but the laws which govern it are immutable and impartial; the methods for voyaging however, can be quite unexpected. Many voyagers have stumbled across what look like *non sequitur* combinations which provide access points.

The apparent unrelatedness of the bizarre and the absurd results from viewing reality through a narrow primate vision without taking into account the macrodimensional levels, which the lower dimension mirrors only dimly.

Some methods of movement can be discovered by trial and error—the expensive way—others by research—the time-consuming and often misleading way—some by inquiry—about the best way of obtaining unusual answers.

The most improbable shamanic voyagers can be consulted, if we keep an open mind as to the validity and practicality of any information a wild savage like a Tibetan or a Navaho would be likely to supply.

Many other "right combinations" can be found, as a safecracker might find the combination of a safe, or by deduction and induction, an extremely unpredictable method, but one which worked well for the Latakia-pipe-smoking cocaine addict at 221B Baker Street....

Many shamanic labyrinth voyaging techniques are definitely frowned upon by our contemporary culture, although many ancient cultures joyously embraced them, and others are entirely forbidden; almost all are taboo to some degree.

Before we dare to experiment in a well-traveled path that ordinarily needs no experimentation, we should determine that we really are stuck, and that we are not merely experiencing a purely subjective impatience.

If we examine each of the methods used to achieve crossover from the human sector and movement in the maze, we will very quickly discover that all of these have in common the alteration of mood, the rudder by which we steer ourselves through the maze.

Mood, in the negative emotional sense, maintains the occlusion-matrix of the human domain but in the macro-dimensions, we use higher moods represented as various forms of love, not in the primate sense, not the single emotion ordinarily associated with biological attraction and rutting desire, but an entire spectrum of new emotion in thousands of forms, degrees and boundless definitions.

Macro-dimensional mood-building occurs quite apart from any nervous system alteration or bio-electrical enhancement as found in meditations. *Macro-mood is not the result of bio-physical effects.* It is far superior and senior, but it may eventually show some effects on the biological machine of a well-seasoned voyager who really cooks in the higher dimensions.

The selection of co-voyagers, a crew, is based partly on what sector of the labyrinth we may need to access, and partly on aptitude, which would include tolerance of higher levels and the events we would be likely to encounter, and hopefully pass through.

A special assembly of varying typicalities can produce quite different and very visible voyaging results; an individual of one typicality cannot be brought to certain parts of the labyrinth that another typicality could easily handle, but working with a team of three, four, five . . . as many as eight voyagers, representing various levels of macro-being, can provide access to otherwise inaccessible labyrinthine sectors.

New voyagers' reflex reactions to entirely unfamiliar reality structures and new dimensional morphologies must be thoroughly tested in a safe atmosphere, a sector not too far removed from the primate level, where, no matter what happens, we know not too much damage is likely to result.

In this light, we can see a definite need for serious training toward better reactions and intuitional solutions to puzzles.

If we go back to our lab rats, we will notice that rats who achieve maze-brightness rapidly also tend to do rather well in situations not directly related to old problems, and that rats who do not achieve maze brightness are incapable of the same training and, using the term rather loosely, discipline.

Rats who achieve maze-brightness rapidly are also capable of *untraining, unlearning* — an important part of learning, particularly in rapidly shifting reality structures— while rats which do not achieve maze-brightness show no evidence of the ability to unlearn previously acquired skills and behavioral habitude.

Unlearning is a very important and powerful prerequisite to relearning. To relearn essentially means to empty an established neural pathway of its existing imprints in the form of favored synaptic connections, and then to develop a new set of intentionally programmed imprints super-imposed upon the same neural pathway. As roshi Basho would say, you can't pour more tea in the cup until it's empty.

Without aptitude and attitude nothing further is possible. From that point on, if one has aptitude and doesn't tend to react violently to the unexpected; if one can learn to take risks, and the biggest risk of all is to wait and see, to do nothing — if one can be trusted implicitly, *without the slightest shred of doubt,* not to betray oneself, then one may be accepted as a co-voyager in more dangerous, radical and unexpected conditions.

Having been through the labyrinth thousands of times myself, I've certainly come to know what to expect, but you can't prepare others by explanation alone; no amount of preparation really does much more than exploit good characteristics already present in a voyager; either one reacts well to the macrodimensions, or one doesn't.

**The more deeper we go,
The harder it be
To decode
So many a message.**

CHAPTER 5

Neural Network Projections

Our knowledge of the environmental world is entirely dependent upon synaptic processing of organic perceptions which come to us at the speed of light; still, this is not fast enough to be in the present; bypassing these organically bound perceptions can provide us with the possibility of direct unfiltered views of the real world, unencumbered by the brain and its significances.

Consider the brain, ignoring for the moment the various nervous systems which are properly part of this lower organic mental apparatus; the brain can be likened to a small, complex labyrinth resembling a three-dimensional matrix composed, among other things, of neural pathways which have been cut by time and usage through soft, slimy gray matter known as the cerebral cortex.

The brain can be viewed as a veritable ocean of probability in a sea of uncertainty and from this view, the probability is that any neural pathway is as likely as any other.

Electrical energy passes through the brain in a series of decreasing options, each neural grouping acting as a branch of an inverted tree.

Energy in the form of electricity and heat enter at the trunk, descending into the larger upper branches, eventually forced by decreased options into one or another of the median branches and then smaller and smaller branches, twigs and leaves, until it comes finally to rest, because it has run out of choice-points; this is the same as if entropy.

Within the brain we find, if we have the equipment—and the stomach—to look for it, certain positive electrical potentials—openings which, like chemical valences, favor the passage of negative electrical energy and, correspondingly, each grouping of negative electrical energy has waveform, electrical morphological topology and, because it has form, tends to favor one pathway over another, modified by chance under the direct supervision of probability distribution over the localized field.

Each twisting and turning in this three-dimensional branching system represents a corresponding twisting and turning in the giant labyrinth called Creation and, in this sense, the brain is a unique type of mirror, a reasonably complex analog simulation system.

At any given moment, we perceive the domain which we currently occupy—taken as a line-of-sight horizon boundaried system, meaning, whatever we can see at the moment, and the events which unfold in it in a way which conforms exactly to a specific view of reality presented to our subjective central neural positioning within the brain of the human biological machine.

Reality as we ordinarily perceive it is determined by only that part of the neural networking which happens to be momentarily active; because we are in a particular portion of the neural network, we project its significance into the environment; the neural network provides us with whatever significance we happen to devise for ourselves to explain the external reality.

In addition to that we have specific ways of organizing our perceptions corresponding to what is commonly called a "headset". Headset will influence who we seem to be to ourselves—our self-view—which, in turn, must as a matter of course profoundly affect our sense of where we are, what we choose to perceive, how we understand our actions, and our impression of the meaning of what we're doing. A headset comes prepackaged with a self-contained set of associations, past experiences, habits, genetic imprints, and beliefs, carried forward by the plodding momentum of organic habit.

In this sense, as we voyage through the labyrinth, it is not so much that we experience dimensional transitions—it is more accurate to say that we actually remain in the same location in view of the fact that *dimensions are all contained in the same space*, and that we experience a change in headset, in the amount of perception we are able to perceive and process, modified by the increase or reduction of brain-created occlusions, determined by our momentary state which in turn is determined by a variety of modifiers the cataloging and conscious control of which have eluded philosophers, educators, psychologists and stressed-out executives for countless centuries.

In the real world, we are always in the same chamber, which when viewed through varying subjective perceptual filtrations gives us the impression that we voyage unaccountably from one dimensional level to another, alternately seeming to experience expanded and contracted space, modified by variable time frames.

When we change headset, an experience which—to the attentive voyager—immediately translates into a change of dimension, it is more than just our perspective which changes. The alteration of our point of view is so profound and so radical that it goes far beyond a new found ability to think in new categories. A change in headset is practically equivalent to a brain transplant or a brain bypass.

Changing headset is a basic prerequisite, a beginning exercise which prepares us for serious voyaging in the labyrinth, leading us eventually to discard all acquired primate ninedencies, tendencies and even elevendencies . . . .

The imposition of primate imperatives upon perception and reaction can only serve to impinge upon higher experiences and distort them, and we'll learn to use various means to ensure that in the macrodimensions, the primate is well-anaesthetized.

If, on the other hand, we are relatively free from the human headset, we are able to position ourselves anywhere in our internal neural network and project this positioning upon our present perceptual surroundings, and in this way project ourselves into one or another part of the labyrinth.

We have, for all practical purposes, found a means of genuine teleportation, of *jaunting* in the Besterian sense, which is to say, our relative positioning within the field of external reality can be made subordinate to our subjective positioning within the neural patterning of the electrical field which we call the headbrain.

Neural network projection is just a pseudo-scientific gobbledigook way of saying that we exist only in the world we perceive, not the world which is actually there, that we live in a totally subjective holographic brain-projection, a dim analogic reflection of the real world.

Imagine the world as an ocean at the edge of which the human biological machine stands like a lonely lighthouse on a rocky cove, its eyes acting as reverse beacons; we who live in the darkness of the brain can never see the ocean, but, through the eyes of the lighthouse, we are able to know something of the outer world.

The brain is itself deaf, dumb and blind, only able to see, hear and speak in the sense that it sends and receives secondary electrical impulses to and from the outer senses, which are carried by a sort of neurological bicycle messenger along connective nerve fibres to and from the brain.

In the black, neural-node-star-studded, as-if indeterminately distant reaches of the brain's interior universe, they are converted to a limited simulation of what the senses perceive; that is to say, the eyes of the biological machine are optical instruments, but we never actually see the optical effect.

The headbrain, cut off from the outside world, encapsulated in the shell of the braincase, remains entirely dependent upon signals passed to it from perceptual organs which really *can* see, hear, feel, smell, and sense because they are in direct contact with the outside world.

The eyes see the real world in the raw, in its almost overwhelming wealth of detail, but they don't have the means, the equipment, with which to recognize anything, they have no discernment to *interpret* what they see.

The same holds true for all organic sensory organs—they are in direct contact but have no possibility of understanding in themselves and no way of processing the information they directly perceive.

It is from these serial bursts of varying voltage coming from the outer senses that the brain is able to construct three-dimensional holographic tactile hallucinations within itself.

It's just a pity that the brain's capacity to generate image happens to be limited by an extremely finite capacity to hold and store information. As we would expect, there is a great deal more out there than the brain can possibly produce in an analog construct; accordingly, it tends to produce a severely cramped shorthand representation of what it sees; no great loss from the primate view; it's a great deal more than what most humans care to see anyway.

Roughly ten percent of the real world is actually taken in and holographically projected in the brain—leaving room for an enormous amount of unexplained—and therefore classified as supernatural—phenomena, stuff that's there all the time, stuff that falls into the realm of information-rejection.

What with oddities suddenly appearing out of nowhere or vanishing just as suddenly to the same place, the headbrain is kept busier than a beaver in a flash flood trying to occlude all the unwanted supernatural data.

The brain cannot live without its holographic representations, and therefore, when it doesn't have any externalized information, it produces its own highly imaginative slightly abstract constructs, continuing relentlessly to produce holographic imagery in the absence of environmental provocation.

Ordinarily, we would have no way of becoming aware that what we see as environment is actually a second-hand holographic projection, sitting as we are, smack-dab in the thick of it all!

The brain does more than project a representation of external reality. It provides us with feelings, sensations and a profound sense of identity within the holographic projection, a subjective impression of ourselves as individuals living at the exact center of a world we have never seen.

We become the central character in the brain, the center of our own little mandala, a miniature Hamlet, miming in silence to the soundless echoes of pulsing voltage, visions of the self, strutting importantly across the stage as the holographic projection rotates past our static observation post.

On the other hand, when the machine is technically in the waking state, the headbrain—which would normally generate continuously updated holographic representations—is automatically disabled, functioning in this state as a motor centrum, which produces the effect of freeing our vision from its normal constraints; our perception of the surrounding world no longer depends upon the headbrain's holographic hallucinations, and we suddenly discover that, because we are able to use our own fairly unlimited attention and are no longer limited to the extremely finite number of attention units of the machine, we can see a veritable wealth of detail we never noticed before.

The real world begins to dawn upon us in the waking state; in the expansion, the environment—including the human biological machine, which is very much a part of the environment—becomes transparent and luminescent, a dew-glistened gossamer web.

As we approach our new life, the life of the voyager, the life of the human biological machine, an illusion of light below the infinite, a residual effect of stillness and silence, seems to disappear, leaving the voyager free to explore the labyrinth.

As the machine awakens, the will of the machine is annihilated producing a transference of will and action from machine to voyager. This is the very first of a long series of transformations which enable us to work in the macrodimensions.

The environment is infinitely more complex than anything the brain can project. The brain is limited to a certain number of symbol references. It only has so much memory, capacity and simulations to work with, and it can't be expected to yield any greater detail in its simulations than the available number of units of attention will allow. The finite number of simulations affords a finite amount of detail and resolution.

We can demonstrate this to ourselves by focusing our attention on one item, observing that the amount of detail formerly perceived in the environment as a whole is now transferred to this single item enabling it to be perceived in greater detail. A magnified view of one item in the environment contains as much information as a wide angle view of a large number of objects—no more, no less.

We may have obtained a few less occluded glimpses now and then as the organic perceptions were short-circuited by various traumatizations. During these experiences, we undoubtedly grasped the fact that ordinarily we are unable to perceive anything approaching the amount of detail actually existing, and that in our ordinary machine state of vertical sleep, we are even further from any exact perception of our true surroundings.

The feeling of frustration when we first saw and understood the stunning severity of limitation of the biological perceptual apparatus must have left a wake of outrage at nature as we came to realize to what extent our perceptions are blunted.

We know that environment suggests brain simulations; the environment also must suggest which portions of the neural networking will accept one of the three major functions; passive, active and inactive...passive, in the sense of a passive tuning fork; active, in the sense of an active tuning fork which when struck can influence a passive tuning fork and make it resonate; inactive, in the sense of a sounding board which contributes nothing to the sound but gives it reverberation and depth.

Glimpses of the real world without the limitations of the perceptual organs of the human biological machine reveal several interesting observations:

The real world only vaguely resembles what we have taken to be the world all along—very vaguely indeed, and not only is the real world far more complex and more detailed than we have taken it to be, but evidently the brain, without consulting us, in its enthusiasm to compress incoming impressions into a manageable mass matching its severe limit of simulation, has distorted and combined many otherwise subtle and elegant perceptions of the real world.

To be sure, it has always managed to simulate the world well enough to allow us to interact, but we never have had the precise picture of how things really are *out there.*

When the brain runs out of attention units for its simulations, it's forced to evaluate detail on a descending scale of priorities, almost all of which happen to fall within the realm of direct or imagined threats to the continued survival of the machine as defined biologically and also, unfortunately, psychologically.

Under that set of priorities, many environmental items do not have a very high priority; the greatest threat to machine survival is, of course, the process of transformation and voluntary evolution, represented by the macrodimensions, portrayed by the brain as "nothingness", clearly marking it "to be ignored and forgotten about"—which, in most cases, takes care of any possible natural curiosity....

As long as we restrict ourselves to interactions with our own brain simulations of the environment, we can only conceive of the labyrinth as a series of subjective phenomena generated within the brain and suggested by the environment, leaving us, for all practical purposes, in the dark about the real world. If we insist on remaining dependent upon the bad guesses of brain simulation, we run the risk of making some very grave mistakes....

We can correlate these interiorized simulations and relegate them to different functionings of the brain, recognizing that one or another brain function has become passive, active or inactive, and therefore seems to propel us into a different part of the maze.

Suppose for the moment that we have bypassed the organic perceptics, and we are for once able to see the real world as it is. Now we see that we have been only a hair's breadth away from it all our lives; we had the eyes, but didn't see; had ears but didn't hear. Now we can see, feel, touch, and *sense* ... oh, how we can sense!

More stumbling than trying,
Increases the likelihood of finding;
To try is to fail,
To *do* is to succeed.

E.J. GOLD, *THE LAST DELAY,* OIL, 24''x18'', 1987.

CHAPTER 6

The Illusion of Time

As we upscale into the macrodimensions, we soon discover that what really prevents us from living macrodimensional life in the timeless, eternal state is our extreme psychological dependence upon the ordinary flow of time as measured by clocks; it is hard to accept time as a function of space and not a linear flow through events.

In the labyrinth, time is meaningless. Objective straight- line timeflow continuum referents are useless here, an intensely subjective and fleetingly momentary experiential level which is soon replaced by an entirely new macrospatial referential set.

Voyaging in the labyrinth, we may involuntarily exhibit staccato movement and other, more internalized reflex reactions which indicate a grimly primate perception of time which we want to see as a predictable continuum of sequentially connected events in an orderly procession of cause and effect.

If we correctly perceive time as a function of space, completely contained in the present dimensional level and perceivable as a spatial dimension in the next higher dimensional level, we will see each existing as a total *Ding-an-sich*, a complete thing-in-itself which has no direct congruent cause-and-effect relationship to any other local continuum event, before or after.

When the information-processing in the brain is accelerated to the level of unobstructed perception at approximate speed of light, it produces what we call the eternalized moment; we experience an event as if it were frozen forever, encapsulated in an eternal suspension.

This introspective impression is entirely subjective; the attention no longer seems to flow along a higher dimensional frame; in this unfamiliar form, time can be seen to be a subtle value-sensing of a next higher dimension, a function of space in the form of an event-horizon.

If we were able to intentionally generate an acceleration of attention in ourselves, the flow of time would, at some point, seem to come to a complete stop and then, quite abruptly, with no segue, we would find ourselves in sudden transition to another eternal chamber—a matrix of macrodimensionality, a transition provoked automatically by more or less the same sort of process of ejection as that of a fetus in a full-term uterus.

When the attention is awake in the higher dimensions, each moment hangs suspended in a subjective eternity which passes only with transition. Macrodimensional attention reveals the true nature of time; it becomes visibly a function of space. What, to our lower-dimensional perspective appears to be succession, is in fact, simple juxtaposition.

Subjective time is linear and accelerated relative to the attention. Objectively speaking, however, time does not actually exist; Creation is a frozen tableau, a class of dimension containing all dimensions.

Time is an objective measurement of the path of the essential self through the Creation—its real path—not the restricted path we think it is, but the full broad path that it actually is.

Real time cannot exist without linear time; linear time is the building block of real time; the two exist at right angles relative to one another.

Linear time corresponds to the passage of the Absolute through the Creation. Linear time is brief in comparison to real time, but linear time corresponds to every new passage of the Absolute.

Real time can be said to be an endless back-and-forth shuttle, an unsubtle repetition unconsidering of detail. Together these two forms of time produce the warp and woof, the woven effect of Creation as a multi-dimensional matrix, planar elements within what is ultimately an empty sphere.

The Creation is crystallized, a solid set of waveforms, a topological figure whose morphology can best be described as some sort of Klein bottle.

Sudden dimensional perceptual changes in the voyager are predictable according to a special form of linear algebra; we move from one moment to the next; transition is almost imperceptible.

The word "moment" in this context, describes a macrodimensional location once-removed from our present state of topological domain, as viewed from below. Moments in this sense are not connected, do not flow automatically, and are not arbitrary divisions of a single flowing thing. A definite transition occurs from one macro-moment to another.

We should not use the words "second", "minute", "day", "week", or "year" in relation to a macroevent; that spatial vector which we perceive as time, measured at right angles to linear time, cannot in this case be said to be just a subjective phenomenon; a transitional event, however, *is* completely subjective, since the macrodimensional domain which we exited remains as it was. The event does not change, just our position within it.

We might experience transition as a blisteringly rapid moment, a fraction of a second or an agonizing trillion-year journey across an endless wasteland within which we seem hopelessly lost and far beyond our ability to endure. From the primate view, we can get caught in the transitions themselves, and become despairing wanderers in the World of Wandering Spirits; this is all an integral part of atavistic shamanic primitivism, but has no place in our practice of nonprimitive shamanism. We can see the lost and wandering effect as a temporary perceptual problem having its remedy in the realization of solutions to the problems of boundary-devouring topological domains.

Measuring temporal phenomena within time itself is simply measuring thirty-six inches with a yardstick. To understand time, we have to find a viewpoint outside it, and when we do, time becomes something very different from what we normally understand it to be.

The end of our lives is the end of infinity from the view of Creation from within the sphere of Creation; we come to the boundary, the wall, on one side of which is decay, old age, death, and on the other, Creation as a finite containment, folded back into itself to produce the apparency of infiniteness, a class containing all classes of time, space and dimensionality.

From this view, the Creation as a topological construct has barriers and boundaries, at the near-point of which, its decaying energy comes to rest, not in a time-frame, but in a permanent matrix, a fixed mathematical level at which we can actually *see* the boundaries; we can watch in amazement as the Absolute bursts through the wall, blazing a trail of morphological presence through the as yet uncut domains of potential attention.

The knowledge we have of the Absolute should not form an attachment to qualifiers, attempts to put the Absolute in contact with, and dependent upon, time and events. Qualifiers can only refer to the Creation. No matter how exalted they appear to us, they are totally inadequate because they attempt to bring the Absolute, a non-dimensional something-or-other, into the apparent context of a time-space continuum.

The example of a Wilson Cloud Chamber can serve to illustrate our knowledge of the Absolute. What we are really describing is a path that was left by the passage of something we can't see or measure; but we can see and measure the collisions and resultant effects upon see-able and measurable phenomena in the wake of its passage.

This gives rise to the impression that the Absolute is perpetually just out of reach, the Tantalus grapes of livingness; and this would be a correct view because our experience of time, our feeling of forward motion, and the memory of our past is like a jet vapor trail; our experience of the present is of that moment at which the vapor trail finally coalesces after the passing of the Absolute.

Always a hair's breadth away, the Absolute always only a single micro-step beyond the most present reach of our presence, that unthinkably immediate living energy—and perhaps much more—which is the cause of all existence.

If nothing particularly unprimate happens, we remain just a trail and nothing further is possible, and yet, because the vapor trail which is our universe has existed, it cannot be erased because entropy is a purely dimensional phenomenon. Under certain conditions, the essential self in the form of a presence unconnected with the dimensional domains can free itself from this decaying pathway of secondary and tertiary energy before it is ground entirely to dust by sheer association and power of suggestion.

It is important that it not just free itself, however, but that it accept an education toward freedom, lest it become a horrible little immortal creature with all the worst aspects of its human primate arisings.

The Work can shape us in a certain way even if we do not fully comprehend the full ramifications of this education; the fact remains that, if we were cognizant of the significance of our continued existence as individuals, we would work with all possible haste and effort to shape ourselves to a work morphology.

The Work is a way of life in the eternal state, following the changes and necessities of the Absolute; this intimacy, this special friendship of the shaman with the living Absolute gives us a clue about where a shaman goes and what a shaman does.

The shaman doesn't voyage out of a vague sense of restlessness, driven on by the same hungers and frustrations that brought the first European settlers to the American

West, and if we aspire to become shamen, we must come to realize that one barrier which really prevents us from living this "life-eternal" as working voyagers in the macro and microdimensions of the labyrinth is our need for relief from boredom, a symptom of our dependence upon the ordinary flow of time as measured by clocks both biological and astronomical.

Accustomed as we are to viewing events as if causally directly connected and linearly sequential, taking our clues for significance from sound, sensation and activity artificially organized by our rigidly formal Euclidean sequential formatted brain, we cannot see that the flow of consciousness is in inverse relationship to the flow of time, which is to say, when consciousness flows, time stops, and when time flows, consciousness obligingly stops.

The technique of easy non-traumatized transition between eternalized moments can transform the process of death, the subjective state which can, if machine-attention is the only form of attention we have developed in ourselves, produce a seemingly endless and unendurable hallucinatory trap during the final few moments of life, into a comfortable and familiar slipping-away from the dock in just another labyrinth voyage, but without the unnecessary burden of the four-dimensional form and consciousness of the human primate.

As we allow our consciousness to accelerate, our subjective experience of life slows down, and we out of necessity are forced to learn a new way of hearing, sensing and seeing; sounds, sensations, emotions, thoughts and actions are at first unbearably slow, and therefore unbearably intense . . . we miss the familiar passage of our old friend time.

At certain times, for certain purposes, it is useful to alter our perception of the space-time continuum. In a school, we work voluntarily to effect specific changes in our temporal perception. This occurs most naturally by an alteration in our temporary dimensional morphology.

One technique of life-extension is based on an intentional use of a higher density of attention to produce eventually a permanent acceleration of consciousness; life is then experienced as isolated, eternal moments which can be transcended by varying rates of passage, for a work-purpose which will become clear as our work proceeds.

Nothing actually changes except the subjective experience of time: sounds become long, low, and impossibly drawn-out . . . The penultimate Southern drawl. Breath may seem periodically—and alarmingly—to stop altogether, while at the same time everything seems alive, illuminated from within and, because the connectivity of presence and all possible points of attention is at unity, without visible distinction between cause and effect.

The passageways and corridors in the labyrinth are actually the transitions across the indefinable boundaries between these eternalized moments. If we could slow down our perception of time, we would easily see that eternity is not the common primate concept—a very long time—but a frozen moment, a vibrating but motionless spatial tableau on a definite and knowable scale of dimensionality having a definite and knowable place in the descending octaves of reality and existence, the lower results of the passage of Creation.

The labyrinth is then viewed as an endless series of eternalized moments — chambers — which constitute the materialized form of the great morphologized mathematical equation which we experience as the Creation.

So, here we are; temporal zombies fixated in artificial primate routines . . . yet we may someday wake up from the walking dead and find ourselves in one or another of these eternalized moments, but it won't just happen by itself.

Because sounds become incomprehensible in the ordinary sense, we must learn a new way to listen, and our attention must extend outward without the usual fragmentation and atmospheric and mentalized scatter.

We must be able to intentionally concentrate, collect, diffuse, place and re-place the attention without dependence on the machine and its superficial skimming form of attention, if it can be called that. Actually, the machine-attention should rightly be termed general-nondirected-machine-awareness.

We must be able to maintain attention on several events at once which occur over a long and seemingly eternal subjective period, in which the low rumbling, hooting, howling, whistling, rolling thunder and progressive jazz harmonies of the macrodimensions are fully understood and dug. A new technique of listening is necessary to enable us to allow these sounds to remain as beautifully, richly incomprehensible and purely musically abstract as they are, in the eternalized state.

We can gain an understanding of this by listening to forms of music, as an example, *Dance of the Hi-Tech Shaman,* as if the instrumental sounds were a human voice speaking conversationally; comprehending it as automatically as if we were listening to someone talking to us, noting in passing as we would conversationally the nuances and colorations, interpreting them just as we would the more familiar verbal conceptual phrasing.

Sensations also present another serious problem for the new voyager; sensations seem to hang forever suspended in quivering, reverberating tensions, apparently endlessly. Oh, sure, with experience, we know that eventually all things will pass; they may even become tolerable ... hasn't happened yet, but one can always hope.

As voyaging becomes more and more familiar and easy, we learn to see and make interpretations in entirely new categories of scale and dimension, finding significance in greater and greater abstracts, tolerating and reacting to them not at all in our primate habitude, but with new attention and a correspondingly expanded point of view.

We have then made the transition from human primate to labyrinth voyager, and none too soon; after all, what business has a primate in the macrodimensions? Like a child suddenly confronted with incomprehensible activities of the adult world, a primate wandering dazed and confused in the macrodimensions will find it impossible to think and behave differently.

To such a primate—and fortunately for them and everyone else, they don't last long in the macrodimensions— it's no crime to throw gum wrappers and crushed beer cans just anywhere that happens to be convenient.

Having achieved a permanent transition to labyrinth voyager, we have the definite ability to make a clear distinction between macrodimensions and the four-dimensional organic world of the human primate so that, even if we might consider trashing the environment now and then, we certainly wouldn't do it in the macrodimensions.

And what of thought? Even extremely high-speed brain-events become painfully slow, unfolding laboriously in unbelievably elaborate automatically evolving snowflake-like patterns from their primary beginning to tiny, delicate branches which vanish in fragmentations as the thought reaches the end of its electrical force and gives up its last remaining heat.

Finally, we may feel as if our voyaging has gotten stuck, that we have unaccountably become trapped forever in a temporal suspension and as we follow our concentrated attention in a nose-dive toward some seemingly unbreakable phenomenal fixation, we find ourselves eventually bursting out of the chamber in an uncontrolled and unidirectional expulsion to another chamber, like shit exploding from an armadillo's ass.

An alternative to this is a method of easy voluntary transition from one chamber to another. However, the boundaries of macrodimensional chambers are not always so easily defined, and occasionally even the most adept voyager is likely to be vomited unceremoniously across the void.

Ritual is the basic recognition of elements of a chamber, those invocational instruments which can be utilized by a voyager to make intentional transitions.

The attentive voyager soon discovers that each chamber contains within it all those invocational instruments necessary to work within the chamber, to understand what is needed, and when the shamanic work is completed for the moment, to produce expulsion and transition to another chamber or dimensional level.

Each chamber, depending upon how rapidly consciousness accelerates, may actually seem like an endless eternity which will never change, and from which we will never escape. A remedy for this dreary view of eternity is rightly the province of work on self.

A key for extended life as a voyager in the labyrinth is to accelerate the higher attention and its totalized awareness until each frozen, eternalized moment, extending inward and outward simultaneously, is suspended in time—all activity, sound and sensation poised in breathless anticipation, an infinite ocean of light in which everything hangs in the balance of stillness and silence, and then try to drink a cup of tea in that position.

An eternalized chamber is not defined by movement through space, the ordinary definition of time. Movement produces an apparent variation in the space and event, *altering consciousness by altering the reference-points of consciousness,* in light of which consciousness automatically redefines itself.

Consciousness in the macrodimensional sense is a product of accelerated attention where the morphology of presence tends to structure itself in a way which may have suggested itself by the present chamber.

To the accelerated consciousness, time slows down and we seem to become encapsulated in totally isolated chambers, frame by frame, like a film held at arm's length, viewed outside a projector or on an editing machine. The next moment has no connection, no memory of the moment before, unless we have trained ourselves to carry our memory past the short-term memory erasure which produces the effect of a veil between one chamber and another.

If we can only remember that short-term memory erasure is a definite factor of transition, it is possible to carry the memory of one temporal chamber into the next. Just remembering that there is memory erasure is generally sufficient to break the veil and recover the memory. This memory-jog is a loosely adapted variation on the Heisenberg Uncertainty Principle, in which observation alters the thing observed, just as a certain type of well-directed attention placed unremittingly upon the machine has a definite effect on the human biological machine, forcing its transition from biological to transformational functioning.

When we have this eternalized vision of life as a labyrinth, we can easily make the transition from one chamber to another in non-linear time without the feeling that we must somehow rejoin the flow of time and regain the ordinary significance of organized linear experience, straight-line associative thought, sound related to distance, action and objects, and sensation related to recognizable organic environmental and internalized mental-emotional and physical body-events.

In the timeless eternity of the macrodimensions, cause and effect occur simultaneously; everything seems connected, events occur at the same moment we happen to think of them, external extensions of our moods and thoughts; we are so attuned to events that we seem to be creating them in the moment. We may become enamored with this idea and fall into a peculiar fascination, a glee game, with a world which seems to reflect every nuance of our internal workings.

This misleading self-mythology is really just a function of the acceleration of consciousness filtered through our ordinary primate vanity. Ordinarily we are not so rapidly attuned to events that we perceive them as they actually occur.

How can we actually learn to accelerate our consciousness to experience this new form of life? When we leave behind us the ritualized trappings of primate life, and begin to live as labyrinth voyagers, only then will we understand what mystics have been trying to tell us for tens of thousands of years. But nobody living below the speed of light—which is stillness and silence—can ever really understand the nature of labyrinth life.

At every turn we have the option to fall back asleep into our old life, that unconscious state which goes hand-in-hand with the ordinary consensus flow of time and its close companion, the pursuit of immediate primate gratification. Of course, now that we have tasted even a little of the life of the labyrinth voyager, our old primate life will seem dead and empty.

**All of life
Is a struggle
Against eternity.**

E.J. GOLD, *MACRODIMENSIONAL RESTROOM,*
UPSTAIRS AT THE GRAND OPERA HOUSE,
PEN & INK WASH, 7''x5'', 1975.

CHAPTER 7

The Mystic Vision

The veil is not in the mind, but in the heart. Only the heart will lift the veil. When this happens, when we have softened and ripened, we will find ourselves to be at the very Heart of the Labyrinth, for which we have longed all our lives.

In reality, we already have a life on a macro-dimensional level, although we may not be aware of it, nor how to take advantage of it. In any case, verification will come from our voyages through the labyrinth which will soon lead us to ascertain for ourselves that *we cannot go where we are not already* and that our potential presence in the macro-dimensional defines the sum totality of our whole possible spectrum of reality.

Having made the transition to labyrinth voyager, one comes to see and recognize one's own multi-dimensionality, and, outward bound from a lower dimension to a higher, one can see how the topological connectivity of macro-dimensional chambers is provided by morphological corresponding to the macro-inhabitant.

In the stillness of the macrodimensions, we progressively come to question the very existence of lower dimensions; they seem dreamlike, something contained in the deep subconscious of the voyager, false memories of spatial and temporal experiments that never really happened, a temporary escape from eternity into the fantastic.

In the macrodimensions, one is, and here one remains, in a single chamber containing all eternity, the duration of Creation a single breathing cycle; for the voyager, bound in Creation, descended from the totality of all possible attention, things take on a strange, new and semi-awesome light; crawling impossibly, maddeningly slowly through a dark and cryptic labyrinth.

Suddenly, in this light, the most incomprehensible reports of mystics become glaringly obvious. There it is, staring us right in the face!

Mystics, both knowing and unknowing, voluntary and involuntary, are destined to perpetual frustration if they attempt to communicate to others their visions.

Many voyagers have returned to tell the tale, to this little corner of the labyrinth in which human primates huddle together in fear of a darkness that will never come, but the knowing voyager will be sealed in silence, reduced to awkward, mental-symbolical verbiage far below the stunning brilliance of the actual vision; not visions in the hallucinatory sense, but full-blown tactile experiences every bit as vivid and tangible as anything in the course of ordinary life— maybe even a little more delineated, more strongly and broadly drawn, much more alive and richly, astonishingly detailed. Ordinary life appears dull and colorless when compared to the depth of experience in these extra-dimensions.

We might be told that we will exist beyond space and time, be absorbed by thoughts, re-live the creation of the universe, see macrodimensional creatures on an unthinkably enormous scale; view the whole universe in a matchbox, and other immense wonders; but to the primate, this is all meaningless, because straight-line pseudo-rational information cannot convey the overwhelming emotional impact of the experience and the utter psychic and personal havoc created by the overwhelming onslaught, the sheer majesty, of Creation in the raw.

Therefore it is not without some dread that we must resolve to continue our dangerous explorations no matter how safe they may appear. It demonstrates a healthy respect for reality to understand the perilous risk, the sheer danger of what we are trying to accomplish. Not a game for dilettantes....

Should we accidentally happen to unwittingly discover a means of access to macrodimensions, it is only natural to try to find out as much as we can and hope for the best. We can act on the assumption that if we can access macro-dimensions, then we rightfully belong there, that we have some sort of natural existence in those dimensions and can somehow make a place for ourselves by arising from our somnambulent state, waking from lower dimensional dreams and learning to become useful and responsible, with regard for our fellow macro-chambermates.

We cannot go where we are not already; properly, we do not voyage from the lower dimensions to the higher, we awaken to find ourselves in the macrodimension, where we always were, shaking off for the moment the nandi-like coils of occlusion which kept us in dreams; the nature of the occlusion is the dream-state of the lower dimensions, a reflexive response to our intolerance of our eternal, unchanging and inescapable—except in dreams—macro-dimensional life.

And here we find ourselves, in the world of our sleeping escape, surrounded by the many strange and primitive creatures which populate our dreams. There is a radical difference between macrodimensional voyagers who have learned to live in the eternal state and those who are content to fall into, remain enslaved to, and rut around in, the primate world, and a similar disparity exists between events higher and lower dimensional. Identifying more specifically the rejective reflexes which lead the macro-dimensional being into the distractions of the downward spiral will be of interest to us only after we have firmly established a place for ourselves in the macrodimensional domain and have gained greater familiarity with our reactions to the eternal visions.

Finding one's way around these macrodimensions is no more difficult, after some practice, than finding one's way around an average contemporary high-density primate city, without being able to speak the local dialect... This can further lead us to an urgent need to know what we can become, and where, exactly, we can become it.

Most people think of maze-bright professional and semiprofessional voyagers as superhuman gurus, individuals to trust and to follow blindly or semi-blindly.

The fact is they aren't superhuman, nor can we take maze-brightness as a guarantee that they are even slightly beyond the hungers of the average primate; sure, somehow they've become aware of the maze, perhaps even learned to play in it somewhat, but macrodimensional experience without the foundation to support it yields nothing; you can throw a monkey into a roomful of computers and it'll still be looking for a banana.

Voyagers who have become visible in the primate world may have developed a more or less complete memory of the maze and may know it intimately, but this is one bet on which I wouldn't give generous odds....

Once in a while in the course of ordinary life, the dimensional veil is lifted and we find ourselves in the Palace. We discover ourselves, hearts open and achingly receptive, sitting at the center of the labyrinth, in a Palace of incomparable beauty and grandeur; we realize that we have been here all along because the Kingdom, the macro-dimension of all possible attention and presence, is always at hand.

We all have recollections—waking and dreaming, vivid and vague—of the Palace. How regrettable that we should experience any distance at all between ourselves and the Palace—but we have to live with the sad fact that where we think we are is where we think we are!....

The Palace is not a symbolic metaphor, but a state of unobstructed vision, revealed when we have reduced the occlusion of our impaired sight and regained our attention to a much higher degree; all us mystics who have seen the Vision of the Palace seem to note the same items: although the structure of the chamber remains essentially unchanged, its lack of size-and-volume definition suggests a Roman palace a shade on the shinier side of pearly; an impossible expanse of rising planes, glistening with brilliant internal clarity provided by increased attention, its finer perceptual resolution resulting in a general effect of polished marble, onyx and lapis lazuli; in the center, what the casual and disoriented observer would most probably call a throne, surrounded by concentrically arranged clusters of individuals, each of whom seems to be totally involved—running to downright befuddled—with the performance of an incomprehensible task involving sound, action and mood, to the exclusion of all else, which we can intuit is intended to somehow support the existence and power of the throne, God alone knows how and why.

This comparison to a Roman palace is not as strange as it may at first seem; Roman palaces were copied from Greek architectural structures which, in turn, were attempts to represent the macrodimensional "ideal"...the abstract archetype perceived by voyaging Greek oracles at a time when they actively sought—and found—macrodimensional vision and knowledge.

The oracles did their best to communicate their visions of the macrodimensional domains in what was to them familiar Olympian symbology, which inspired architects to erect structures modeled after these partly unveiled labyrinthine visions.

Palaces in fairy tales, Norse mythology and Eastern shrines and temples were obviously suggested by the perception of the real world. The Ice Palace and the Crystal Palace also refer to this structure at the center of the macrouniverse. Spenser's Kingdom of Faerie also originates in this idea. The macrodimension is something with which we're intimately familiar, but to which we can't seem to open our perceptions.

Some of us may from time to time catch momentary spasmodic and involuntary glimpses of this in dreams or waking visions—sudden perceptions of unusual clarity, and now, having caught such glimpses, we are training ourselves for the voyage into the Palace, from which we may someday make a permanent crossover into the Kingdom, the macro-dimensional domain of the Work.

We don't recognize our presence in the higher dimensions not only because of psycho-emotional barriers, which we examined at length in relation to the perception of higher dimensions in *The Human Biological Machine...,* but because of vestiges and momentum of human primate habits which prevent us from using our full attention and manifesting our complete presence.

If we expect to work every day at a wholesale meat market, and one day abruptly drop dead, we may very well find ourselves preparing the next subjective day to, according to habit, report for work as usual.

We might now be in the Palace, but we don't think so; our actions reveal someone who acts like a primate in a wholesale meat market.

As we become aware of our presence in the macro-dimensional, something about us will be slightly different; a subtle nimbus, a comparatively dim effulgence—dim, when taken in relation to the general fluorescent atmosphere of contemporary urban and suburban supermarket sources of carcinogenic radiation—of personal atmosphere generated around us when we fully realize that we *are* in the Kingdom, will serve as a signal that tells the average macro-dimensional observer that we're "on", that our presence is attuned to the macro-state.

But deep within us are all the propensities to perpetuate the primate cloud of unknowing; we are like *Pigpen* in the *Peanuts* cartoons, a character unknowingly surrounded by a perpetual cloud of dirt, mud, flies, and dust, a moving mass of particles of filth, attracted to him by sheer

habit—the quality of "charm" in quark-to-quark relationships—in the same way a steel needle repeatedly stroked by
a strong magnet becomes aligned, and is temporarily
polarized; it could be said to have become a magnet by sheer
habit.

Our most solid human primate views and concepts,
beliefs and attitudes, perceptions and fixations are attached
to us in the same barnacular way.

We've got a permanent Pigpen plexiform surrounding
us—dirt, flies and dust—hanging around us. Even in the
Palace, the veritable Heart of the Labyrinth, we've not yet
cast off this outer garment which clouds our vision and
which, unless we cast it off and redress ourselves in the white
shameless garment of the wedding-guest, will force the heart
to squeeze us out of itself, to reject our unclean primate
presence, the presence of an angry, bewildered, self-
pampered hairy little ape, wreaking havoc and leaving
behind us a trail of wreckage.

In a sense, our own ability to see and understand what
is actually going on at any given moment is completely
irrelevant, because the effects of the labyrinth are electrical
and independent of significance as we ordinarily understand
it.

If we seriously expect to penetrate our vision past the
clouded occlusion of the visual senses, we must enter another
perceptual level, the secret vision of the mystic, who allows
sensation to suggest interpretation of the vision. We can use
this secret in an exercise to reveal and develop the higher
emotional centrum and higher mental faculties, bringing us
ever-deeper and more dangerously into the domain of the
shaman, the playful participant in the self-generative cyclic
dance, the *Leela*, of the majestic *Shakti*, energy in the raw.

Visioning, the shamanic way of seeing, requires that
the eyes—not the organic eyes of the primate, but the vision
of the directed attention of our collected morphological
presence—be unveiled and, for these special shamanic eyes
to open, we must use the heart, not the mind, with which to

think; the veil of occlusion is held in place by the cold heart of primate fears. This is no great shamanic secret!

Visioning can give us perceptual access to the macro-dimensions, but actual presence in the macrodimensions requires the activation and understanding of the heart, the higher emotional centrum which alone—but only when it's alone—is capable of producing the exalted mood necessary for access into the Palace, the Heart of the Labyrinth, and wrapped around our presence like a mantle or a shroud, keeps us safe and warm on our voyages into the coldest, most far-flung outer reaches of the labyrinth.

The rejective obstructions to visioning and performing our macrodimensional work are the same things that keep us imprisoned on the human level, all those primate-ive considerations, problems, and unfounded and unexamined beliefs that have formed in us and solidified into rigid electrical barriers which automatically direct and control our actions, and maintain the lower emotional attitudes and self-oblivion . . . .

Unknown and unviewed beliefs color our attitudes and filter our vision; everything is taken in through this filtration system and restructured into a shadowy conforming attribute.

Fixated beliefs have an effect on everything we see, distorting things in one particular direction. Anyone who voyages through macrodimensions discovers hidden assumptions, attitudes and beliefs operating covertly—silently and invisibly influencing all one's perceptions and decisions.

The voyage to the Heart of the Labyrinth is our first real initiation into the Work. *It is the Heart of the Labyrinth which forms the gateway to any journey.* From here, even the most remote sectors of the labyrinth are within easy reach.

It is here that we will be cleansed by the harsh, intense, distortion-free and unveiled radiation of love, raw energy in its Absolute form, of our remaining primate contaminations; we are purified, made clean, baked by radiation, slowly—excruciatingly, agonizingly, achingly slowly—purified, cooked little by little, each time we pass through the Hearth of the Labyrinth . . . .

The journey to the Palace, the Heart of the Labyrinth, always occupies the key place in traditional shamanic teachings. We need only soften, ripen, mellow with age, open ourselves to it without reservation, without thought for ourselves, of what will become of us.

We cannot rip the veil away with our hands, we cannot pry it off with even a surgeon's sensitive fingers; nor can we remove it with the mind. Indeed, the more we try, the more distance and alienation we place between what we are seeking and ourselves. In this macrodimensional quest, the mind is of no assistance; it isn't part of the world we are after; the mind belongs to the world of the machine.

When our eyes finally open to visioning, it's only because we have intuited some way—a way known only to ourselves and to those others who have found it in themselves—to circumvent a handicap which has woven itself so inextricably into our own hearts that it has become all-but-invisible; it finally gives way only to our most attentive self-observation.

Only the heart can lift the veil. But the machine's reaction to the open heart is very painful. We must learn to live with this pain and with the reactions of the machine until our machine conditioning has been dissolved in a special kind of hard-radiation therapy at the Heart of the Labyrinth.

As the higher emotional centrum becomes active, we will experience new emotions; we may be quite familiar with very intense machine emotions, but we are not at all familiar with moods of the essential self which are neither negative, nor positive. Real emotion has been called love, but this love has no resemblance to what we ordinarily know of or think of as love.

A certain type of sentimental, maudlin emotion can be confused with the real emotion, love. But the two are light-years apart, though to a primate, the difference is indiscernible, or would be, if the higher were available. sometimes by accident, it is; few primates survive the trauma, yet have no idea what particular brand of lightning struck them down.

Higher emotion is unable to respond to machine emotions because the negative electrical flow of machine emotions obstructs the flow of macrodimensional love. The machine can generate powerful emotions that might be similar in their effects to the effects of labyrinthine love, with the exception that they are wiped out in the presence of higher radiations. Love not of the machine is not comprised of hungers and cravings, is not generated by machine-primate needs, wants, and desires, and responds well to the cleansing radiations in the Heart of the Labyrinth.

The machine distorts real perceptions and ideas to its own purposes, and is thus capable of producing and finding satisfaction in simple primate eroticism and pornography. Higher dimensional love is devoid of such childish and superficial corruptions of the attention.

Adoration with total attention which is a form of macro-dimensional love sometimes activated in the process of serious—and often dangerous—shamanic lovemaking which, believe me, is nothing like what you're thinking of trying tonight if you can find a willing partner . . . can often further amplify the pain of separation so profoundly felt by anyone truly in love, which is to say, absorbed in and by the presence of living love, the invisible consciousness and presence which human primates ignorantly call "God".

Were we completely able to relax in lovemaking, opening and devouring the object of attention into our inner stillness and quietude of presence, we might occasionally note a slight tremble which could possibly indicate to an outside observer that we are experiencing this yearning adoration.

In the ordinary process of primate lovemaking, the more subtle higher emotional moods and realizations are somewhat submerged in the urgency of ganglia-directed thrusting and humping.

Higher emotion when it impinges on the machine may cause severe heartburn—a technical term for that sweet aching, that longing for what we are already a part of—and the more such pain we feel, the more we know that we are on the right track, nearer to the ultimate origin of species.

The pain is our direction-finder to the heart. Of course, for those who wish to avoid feeling the raw, raging power of love, there are many ways to avoid the pain: eating is a well-known and regularly used substitute for just about anything; shopping is also a very effective means of distracting ourselves from these deep, gnawing feelings. Movies are an all-time favorite for getting away from everything in general.

Why do we feel so much pain? The machine is covered with electrical anomalies—geodesic warts, so to speak, much like those found on a toad, and the radiation we expose ourselves to in the Heart of the Labyrinth, the cleansing radiation of love, acts as a slow wart-removal medicine, dissolving the warts a little at a time.

The warts act rather like primate-level psycho-emotional hooks which when scraped or caught on the rough-textured surfaces of labyrinthine experiences, cause shock and pain, a discouragement sufficient for most new voyagers, the larger percentage of whom will give up and return to their former primate lives ... and keep their precious warts.

Hopefully most of our lower-dimensional warts will have been removed through repeated exposure to the cleansing radiations of the higher dimensions by the time of primate death, because at terminus we will be exposed to such an intense acid-dip of heavy radiation that all of our warts will be removed at once. If we are not already wartless, dead in this sense, having died before we die, our sense of self-presence and self-directed attention which makes us useful in the Work of higher dimensional voyaging will be utterly destroyed in the process.

As voyagers, we are constantly exposed to cleansing radiation at each pass through the Palace, but it has no salutary effect unless our warts are fully exposed, opened to dissolving radiation by the special pain of adoration centering in the heart.

If we refuse this cleansing, however discomforting, we are wasting our time on earth. When we feel the special higher emotion as it causes pain in the organic heart, we say that "our horns are showing", which means that we are at the moment vulnerable to the cleansing radiation of the higher dimensions.

If we don't know this pain of yearning, nothing can be done for us. If we have to ask the direction to the heart then we are still far too submerged in the primate to see and understand the work of higher dimensional voyaging.

The closer to the heart, the more the pain's intensity. Eventually, like Lawrence of Arabia, we learn that the trick is not avoidance, but in not minding the pain.

We can use the sensation of pain as our beacon, our direction-finder. The more intense, the closer we are to the Heart of the Labyrinth. This idea of the directional use of emotion is similar to the use of the sensations associated with the "chronic" in the intentional awakening of the human biological machine in its use as a transformational apparatus.

**The secret
Is not minding
The pain.**

E.J. GOLD, *HE WAITS VERY ATTENTIVELY, BUT FOR WHAT?*
OIL, 24''x 20'', 1987.

CHAPTER 8

Lightning Handlers
Always Crackle

We work to develop what remains after personal annihilation, because only that is truly able to work! To understand love is to dissolve the self and the subjective mysteries of appearances into it.

In the macrodimensional space, voyagers are able to perceive themselves as thoroughly connected appendages of one single body from which one must separate, isolate, sever the subtle connections, in order to be able to say "I love you" without laughing right out loud.

In technical shamanistic jargon, "I love you" is a comment not unlike what a shuttle captain might announce: "we have ignition", "we have lift-off", "all systems nominal", or "uh-oh" . . . .

"I love you" is a topological fact which refers neither to a relationship between two beings, nor to an activity occurring between two or more organic forms; "I love you" indicates bifurcation, separate identities, morphological mitosis, momentary or otherwise.

To a shaman, love can be seen as a continuously existing substance; a shaman doesn't fall in and out of love. It doesn't come and go like a disease.

Real love implies serious risk, and risk, in the work sense, means to take chances outside the human dimension—sometimes correctly calculated, sometimes not. We take risks for the sake of love, love the eternal substance, the living presence which humans have always thought of as their god, before which no creature can stand and fail to be annihilated; the shaman cares nothing for love the primate ideal, or love the biological attraction.

Love is the very object of adoration, a form of eternal, nonconvertible energy as necessary to our work as heat is to chemical change, or electricity, steam or gasoline are to mechanical engines.

We ought to be able to allow love to ebb and flow, to move freely through us without the slightest quiver of resistance as we would allow the passage of any other form of energy and radiation. If we are to work effectively, we must not let our natural primate fear of the raw force of love be a barrier to the living presence of the Absolute.

A natural fear of the raw presence of love is a very powerful instinct, and a profound problem for the neophyte shaman. Often one doesn't know how to identify the fear; it may cause some embarrassment, shame or humiliation, eventually producing in oneself a definite apprehension, one might say, a fear of fear.

As human primates, we were taught the pretense that we are capable of generating love, that we are a source of love and that we are able to produce it at will and send or receive it as we would a candy-gram.

This human fantasy is wildly inexact. What we generate and send to someone falls into the general category of maudlin and sentimental primate imperatives. We send sentimentality to someone—senti-ment—the combination of sensing and mental, and they send us something back in return—something like a negative-emotional Hallmark card minus the postage.

It is neither desirable nor possible to entirely eliminate fear, especially the fear of love, and we might never overcome the automatic squirming spasm which arises in any primate who happens to fall under the intense, inexorable flow of the raw force of love, but we can learn to work within the energy field we call "love" and, with serious training, perhaps even learn to like it. We can think of love as just a dreadful inconvenience with which a shaman can learn to live.

We don't want to interfere with our natural reactions so long as in spite of our fear-reactions, we do not disturb the flow of energy or interrupt our work in the presence of the Absolute.

We don't know how much effort or energy it will ultimately require, but we mustn't allow ourselves the luxury of sinking into our thoroughly instilled primate fears; we can make it through; we know we can, because we've been doing this shamanic business for an uncountably long time, and we're still here to tell the tale.

As shamen, we ought to be concerning ourselves with the development of a relationship with the force of love itself—not a relationship through love, or a love relationship between rather urgently mating primates.

We are told, not nearly often enough, that the Absolute is love, so a relationship with love ought to work out as some sort of direct relationship with the Absolute. We don't know much about this yet, and might not know what it really means for a long time; just a temporary relief, you can be sure.

We will find in our voyaging that we can't go someplace where the Absolute is not, nor even someplace where the Absolute is more present than another place; in the same way, we can't find a refuge which offers the absence of love, because the presence of the Absolute and the living force called "love" are one and the same.

We can perhaps comprehend the shamanistic idea of risk when we compare the uninterrupted flow of love to floating underwater with an open mouth. When we open to the presence of love we'll surely drown, die before we die, because love kills—love is the ocean of a single drop within which the world is contained.

Everything is calling at us when we open to the presence of love. Everything wants to absorb us. And we want to dissolve, to dissipate out into it all.

The only safety is in keeping apart, holding ourselves separate from love, remaining primate; we cannot remain human and be in love, at least not the love we mean, the living presence of love.

To be *in* love is to say, to be *with* love, *enceinte,* as a woman is with child; were we then still visible, we'd have become something else, something more than human, extending outward from our human primate morphology, and even though continuously present, we might to the ordinary eye vanish without prior notice at this very moment.

In the same way, unless we are able to differentiate the living presence of love from love the primate activity, love the biological necessity, love the emotional weight, love the sentimental slop, love the maudlin whimper, love the animal sport, love the thing that makes beauty parlors go round, we won't really understand love at all.

Love must be differentiated from the hungers of the human biological machine; primate love, even in its most exalted form, can only hinder our work, because it bars us from the Heart of the Labyrinth, the central chamber which is the key to all our work.

The love upon which we must learn to gaze directly without fear, if we are to ever become able to concentrate our work-attention upon it, is love the presence, and we should know that the higher emotional and mental centrums are both capable of being engulfed by the presence of love and even applying it toward the awakening of the Shekinah, the sleeping Creation, without too much destruction, because in the presence of love, the essential self does not cease to exist—presence does not annihilate presence.

On the other hand, when the machine fully enters the waking state, it opens up to the force of love and we might detect a little sizzle as some of the most recent accumulations of the biological machine are burned away.

In this way, the effect of the waking state is cumulative, because each time we open to the presence of love, a little more habitual ego-self, all the accumulations of the egoistic identity, which are not pure presence, is inevitably annihilated.

The simplest and easiest type of machine-awakening is an awakening of the motor centrum, the next easiest is the mental centrum; but without the higher emotional apparatus, the transformational effect of the waking state is somewhat subdued; the special mood of the waking state is, as we'd suppose, the most difficult awakening to achieve.

This special emotional state, in conjunction with a three-centrumed awakening of the machine, is an essential factor to the transformational functioning of the waking state. In this regard, the importance of repeated exposure to the intense and ineffable presence which is called "the Absolute" or "love" is quite understandable.

We work to develop that pure presence which remains unscathed following self-annihilation; to understand love, to become part of it, dissolve into it.

Using the force of love is like grasping a huge electrical conduit in each hand and allowing the current to pass through us; some part will surely survive... the part that is able to work, but the primate self will not. Of course, even without such intentional repeated shock, the biological will die anyway, but peacefully, quietly, in sleep.

Certainly some part of being able to work involves being a capacitor, accumulating love as an electrical force and then applying it in the form of a gentle prod to bring the Creation out of slumber; love is *la force* of the tarot.

We perhaps think of love as pleasant, nice, beautiful, lovely, marvelous, delightful and pretty. This is an accurate picture of a red-satin heart pasted to a fancy paper doily, but not of love.

If we hope to even have a ghost of a chance, the slightest prayer to become practicing shamen, voyagers with a chance of surviving in the macrodimensions, we will have to go through periodic self-annihilation at various points in relation to the machine, using the force of the presence so that machine obstacles are slowly but inexorably eroded. This is not intended to be something that happens just once in a while, in a weekend workshop.

Various unexpected biological reactions to the presence of love inevitably occur; the shaman doesn't try to conquer those reactions, but remains as calmly as possible exposed to the cleansing radiations of the pure force *love,* taking note of the inevitable fears which seem to spring from nowhere and nothing; spasmodic responses of the self-protective muscle system, and reactions of the unfathomable mind in its interminable slavery to the nervous system, learning to live without these little primate balancing games as they are annihilated one by one, keeping some part of the attention on the idea that we cannot change what is, but we can learn to tolerate and even to like it.

Objective music is a way of processing raw love, bending it, forming it, modulating it in definite ways. It *is* love. Change of pitch, legato, or meter can be likened to bending a plumbing pipe or increasing and decreasing its diameter.

If we understand the mechanics of fluidics, or the dynamic principles behind the flow of electrical force—how electricity is shunted, controlled and used to modulate itself—then we may be able to visualize how a shaman works with the force of love. It is simultaneously the aqua and the duct.

The explosive force of love could be said to resemble a ton-and-a-half of magnesium flares igniting simultaneously in the left front breast pocket; we're then expected to somehow shape and draw it with our bare teeth; turning, twisting, planishing and bending it into useable form.

As professionals, we don't sap out on love; we *use* love, move in love, open ourselves to love, shape it, form it, funnel it, channel it, sculpt it, direct it, intensify it, concentrate and dispel it, and for this we must apply a special type of attention mastered through a special exercise of the will which develops a level of attention far beyond what the average human being would automatically inherit from nature, and how many human primates have access to the *attenticizer*, patent pending?

Attention is the invisible hand with which we can mold love; it is the eyes, ears, arms, hands and voice of the essential self.

We must also know that *love itself is the object upon which we are focused*. Love is like lightning. We must have compassion while handling it, and even compassion for the lightning itself. Compassion is an attribute accessible to, and necessary from, any lightning-handler.

Lightning-handlers high up on the totem pole might be called gods by some civilized machine-age savage because something about them seems to remind them of their primate conceptions of cleanliness and godliness.

The Absolute has a few compassionate aspects, but not by human standards; compassionate, yes, but merciful, considerate, kind, obedient, good, nice, humble, prompt, no. Whatever the Absolute is, it isn't a boyscout, unless a boyscout happens to have exactly the same attributes as lightning; with anything even a little like lightning, we're bound to crackle just a bit when handling it.

As anyone with the slightest personal experience with lightning can tell you, electrical energy is all-pervasive; it can concentrate its potential and expand through space, striking any receptive pocket at any given moment.

If we intend to handle lightning, we are constrained to without hesitation become only that which cannot be lost when lightning strikes, which means that we must be free of the primate morphology, having extended and identified far beyond its biological vulnerability.

Is it really possible for macrodimensional shamen to self-arise from stupid, fearful, weak and delicate, needful self-pampered creatures calling themselves human beings, crawling around on the mucky crust of a little mudball spinning in space at the farthest edge of an obscure spiral galaxy? The absurdity of such a concept must give us serious pause, and without some sort of miracle to give them a spine, heart and deeper perception, we could hope for little more along this line than the sale of a few thousand books.

We must understand that the genuine necessities of cosmic maintenance and higher evolution cannot be understood by such creatures of the primate domain, but how could they be expected to cross the ausable chasm which separates them from the life of a voyager, when only a very small number of them ever have? We strive to become a victim of our own integrity and the sense of obligation to the Absolute.

Lightning partakes of the impartiality of pure energy; it doesn't see or understand the hurt, pain and suffering that mortal creatures endure as a result of the concentrations and explosive flow of its passage.

At the same time, through rational deductive reasoning, the lightning may have at last become vaguely aware of these self-evolving creatures striving slowly, painfully, but always self-importantly through the muck and slime of this and other similar little mudballs.

This work of evolution toward the Work of higher dimensions can be accomplished either by an individual or a group, but a group must be composed of individuals who are really able to share the burden; however, it must be said that a group doesn't de facto diminish the intensity for each participating individual. In this work, there is no safety in numbers. On the other hand, there is benefit to the Absolute when a group, under certain circumstances, operates as a single unit composed of several individuals of varying typicalities.

Imagine a group of plumbers in a chamber which has thousands of inlets and outlets in its walls, and the aim is to run piping throughout the entire room. The plumbers start to take direct lines, but eventually inevitably run out of available space and are forced to take bends, skirting around one another.

The point is, they are not co-creating, but co-engineering. A lightning handler's job *is* more of an engineering task than anything else. "I love you" is an engineering statement much like "We're strapping some-thing to the buss" or "We've got a great bridge here". I/love/you is a notation describing a new morphology, a temporary macrodimensional network hookup...of course temporary...ultimately, they all are.

What is it that enables a shaman to be able to use the force of love without getting damaged, as would a medium or a psychic?

Mediums and psychics do it for fun or for money, playing with raw energy out of sheer ignorance and primate inquisitiveness, and injecting into it their own brand of superstitious numen.

Of course, we'd better be dead before we die, otherwise we're going to get fried just like the medium or psychic. *Nothing stands in the face of the Absolute* . And *nothing*, but a nothing with a functioning presence and attention, is exactly what we'd better become if we expect to get some work done in the vast domains of this great cosmic labyrinth!

Some of our beginning work will therefore consist of those steps necessary to rid ourselves of whatever in us would get fried out by an overdose of God. We're expected to develop some sort of immunity to high-voltage electricity, and the best immunity is total identity, to *become* love.

**Seduction is
Not pulling in
But pushing away.**

CHAPTER 9

The Art and Science of Invocation

All macrodimensional invocation is focused on the activation of corresponding resonators between chambers until they vibrate in sympathetic unison. We also have the ability as a being to self-invoke, to expand our morphology into a space where we are not.

During the past several centuries the word "magic" has become a synonym for superstition and personal occult power, a general expression for something not currently categorizable because it happens, at the moment, to fall outside one or another known category of contemporary science.

But we should not forget, if indeed, we ever knew it in the first place, that yesterday's magic is today's science, the logical consequence of which is that today's magic is equally tomorrow's science.

One of our problems, a legacy of our primate forebears, is the word "magic", used in many different ways, mostly derogatorily, sometimes properly.

In its primary meaning it signifies ritual, not necessarily occultist or religious—and should include all those psycho- emotional instruments and forms which can be utilized by a voyager to make transitions into the macrodimensions, and to be fair, this meaning should be expanded to include all ritualized action, even of a social order, such as weddings, handshakes, Valentine's Day cards, Monday night football and the pledge of allegiance.

In other applications it is intended to suggest that laws of a macrodimension have imposed themselves into a lower dimension, implying that, at present, we do not understand exactly which laws are operating, to which dimension they belong, or exactly how and why they have imposed themselves, especially on us, and always at the most inopportune times.

Sometimes magic is used to mean evocation, the drawing up of a lower dimensional voyager, a part of our inner domain, the world or worlds presently contained within us, into the domain we now occupy, on whatever morphological scale we may happen to be at the moment; or invocation, in which we upscale from a lower dimensional morphology into a macrodimensional morphology; this latter form of magic is that which interests us as labyrinth voyagers, because invocation in its fullest sense refers to the methods by which we upscale into macrodimensional morphologies, which, although they are not alive in the organic sense of the word, can be said to inhabit higher domains; each macroinhabitant having a unique character, activity and will of its own, but only in direct relation to its environmental matrix.

The culturally charged words "magic" and "invocation" can be translated into a more technical language the sense of which was partly conveyed in the chapter on time and space. Stripped of its trappings of pseudo-spiritual taboo, invocation can be said to be based on an alteration of our temporal and temporary dimensional morphology; it is the intentional assumption of a corresponding morphological presence and inhabitation in a macrodimension which is appropriate to or in accordance with the targeted topological domain.

Invocation in its esoteric sense refers to a technique that enables one to access or activate a broad category of phenomena indicating the activation of elements or laws of macrodimensions within the format of lower dimensions, an intrusion into the ordinary of what suddenly appears to be inexplicable and bewildering for any unknowing outside observer. Invocation exerts both fear and fascination over us, only so long as we choose to ignore the macrodimensional quality of Creation, and some of the more readily available techniques for voyaging in the labyrinth.

Virtually any chamber can become accessible by using the technique of morphological shapeshifting corresponding to the topological configuration of one or another macrodimensional inhabitant. An assumption can be defined as taking upon oneself the characteristics, morphological presence of a macrodimensional character—not dissimilar from what an actor does with makeup, costume, posture, gesture, manner and tone.

The less an actor knows of the character, the more he must rely upon makeup, costume, props, clichés, and other elements of equal importance, no one more than any other; any decent actor can invoke a character with just a few deft twists of posture, gesture, tone, expression, and mood and, without relying on costume, make us believe the character.

State, mood, thought patterns, and concentration of thought—all special methods for accessing higher labyrinthine dimensions—can be used to bring ourselves into correspondence with something in the macro, or to bring something into correspondence with our lower, primate selves, if we prefer.

Under this category would fall the invocational use of the laws of similarity and contagion; voluntary suggestibility, popularized in the form of self-hypnosis; and adaptation by mimicry, a time-worn shamanic method of costume and action, such as a bow-hunter in a buffalo robe; all of these operate well within the province of the laws of resonance.

We commonly apply these techniques in our primate lives without being aware of their significance or power. For instance, every Western woman is aware of the power-of-chic . . . clothing, cologne, hairstyle . . . which are intended to resonate with—and evoke suitable responses from—the biological-instinctive male sexual apparatus, and every late teenage human male is well aware of the profoundly attractive power of continual hair-combing, filthy jeans and an aggressive, arrogant, insecurity-based sophisticated sneer.

Ordinary suggestibility can take us quite far along the ordinary primrose path, but if we know how to wrap ourselves in the cloak of macrodimensional suggestibility, we can quickly and cleanly extricate ourselves from the domains of the primate world and fling ourselves into the farthest reaches of the macrodimensional domains.

We can bring ourselves into such close correspondence to any macropresence within a chamber that we are identical to it and, if we are able to concentrate our attention on its more potent resonating factors and if we are reasonably free of the usual primate exaggerated psycho-emotional inhibiting fetters, extend even this macromorphology beyond itself until we are the chamber itself, at which point we find ourselves occupying the form of a resident in the next higher dimension.

It goes without saying . . . I find myself saying that it goes without saying, and then proceeding directly to say, that the greater number of exact resonating factors we can reproduce by mimicry in the lower dimensional morphism, the more exact our morphological correspondence will be to our target macrodimensional figure in the destination chamber.

Considering for a moment the raw mechanics of invocation, any labyrinthine voyager knows instinctively to relax all muscular tensions whenever things get intense, and to leave all primate considerations and reality fixations outside the chamber.

This transitional state is characterized by the total relaxation of all tensions—emotional and physical—however seemingly trivial, followed by the immediate relaxation of all mental tensions, the result of which should be as tangible as the sensations and general effect of ordinary muscle relaxation.

In the motor centrum, the transitional state may be viewed by the uninitiated as a type of trance state, but it isn't a trance; it's just a state of relaxation of the personal will, enabling a concentration of attention and presence.

Only when the will of the primate has thoroughly and tracelessly subsided can the tension of the higher will, the will of the essential self, begin to manifest in voyaging actions.

The neophyte voyager will soon discover that, at the slightest automatic reflex of primate will and consciousness, the macrochamber tends to eject anyone rather unceremoniously the moment an invocation is destroyed, and the artificially superimposed macrodimensional topological configuration and higher mental-emotional state becomes disjointed and broken.

The shamanic voyager who is free of primate reflex passes eventually into a chamber which can be recognized by the following factors: a hushed stillness with a church-like quality; a feeling of isolation and eternal timelessness; a feeling of completeness—the chamber needs nothing outside itself to sustain itself; a hermetic seal through which no unauthorized visitors may pass during its use; every object and every inhabitant of the chamber has a definite place; everyone and everything belongs there and what is not there does not belong there; everything in the chamber is native to it.

If all goes well—a rare occurrence in the higher dimensions—the transition from the organic to the higher chamber is rapidly achieved. Typically, chamber transition is detected by change; change tends to become evident between chambers, not in them.

Once we have settled into a chamber, we have nothing from outside with which to measure; we are forced to measure it by its own yardstick, and nothing upon which to hoist ourselves but our own petard.

The study of chambers seems at first impossibly subtle, but then as familiarity allows elaboration of vision and higher perceptive functions, even exceedingly minor variations become obvious, until only another macrotrivia enthusiast perceiving the very deepest subtleties of the more rarefied atmospheres along the farthest ends of the electromagnetic spectrum is able to appreciate exotica which, even to the most highly trained vision and disciplined attention, is just so much non-Euclidean gobbledegook, in the same way that an Indian raga, to the untrained Western ear, presents a boringly repetitive chordal repetition with little or no variation in the way that it repeats.

At various points, the truly attentive voyager may notice the dim, shimmering presence residing far outside the ordinary visible spectrum, more felt than seen, of a vibratory doorway leading to another chamber or opening into a corridor.

At the exact moment of convergence, the practiced voyager enters the relaxed state allowing a new naturally arising energy tension to produce the transition to the new chamber.

The key to this type of soft transition is intentionally self-produced relaxation at points of electro-magnetic tension, with the understanding that we have at least some vague idea of the path along which we are presently hurtling, even though we may not be able to guess the exact purpose of it until much later, in review, if indeed we ever discover the deeper significance of each voyage. About some voyages we can know a great deal; others, just a hint of their meaning and our effect in the macrodimensions; about the meaning behind some of our voyages, however, we will perhaps never know . . . .

How do we know what to expect and which turns to take? We are expected to concentrate attention not only on the necessities of the chamber itself, answering its governing laws with an instantaneously choreographed extemporaneous response consisting of action, non-action, and some self-initiated initiation, but also on the surrounding chambers, keeping alert for opportunities to make a transition from one chamber to another.

In a systematic—but seldom direct—penetration of macrodimensional veils, we thread our way by a balanced blend of wild instinct and unfounded intuition along the path of slightly less resistance in much the same way that an old, experienced bird-dog finds its way to a quail-shot riddled duck.

We have already seen that both individual and clustered voyagers influence the labyrinth voyage according to individual typicality, a blend of attitude, cultural conditioning, and general emotional tone.

The typicality of a voyager—meaning both morphology and general subjective state—determines the path, opening certain ways and closing others; some voyages require orchestrated clusters of highly disciplined voyagers to produce the necessary complex sequential flow of posture-formations; certain typicalities automatically produce specific configurations which bring us into otherwise inaccessible macrodimensions while other typicalities tend to influence us toward a very different set of morphological correspondence.

This idea has extremely far-reaching consequences upon which we will touch briefly just to indicate the scale of implications.

Topological connectivity in the macrodimensions is provided by morphological identity; something in the macrochamber looks like us—not necessarily the way someone not familiar with the mathematics-physics rules of configuration might think of lookalikes, but according to the laws of mathematical similarity.

"Looks like" indicates that some kind of corresponding configuration exists or can be artificially made to exist, that the lower dimensional morphology is equal to, or "as if" equal to, something in the macrodimensions, an idea with which anyone who has a "lookalike computer" such as an IBM clone will be familiar.

If we connected all those events in which we presently have morphological presence, we would see immediately what it is that determines what we call the life of the machine, which is for the moment, our total path through the Creation until we extend our morphology beyond the human primate configuration.

"Morphology", as we use it, means more than the shape of the human biological machine. It includes the psychological characteristics, dispositions and attitudes, the overall electrical field with all its anomalies and eddies; we will soon be brought to study the eddyology of electrical anomalies.

In the waking state, we realize that the macrodimensional domain is, and has always been, in plain sight, but the focus of attention from the platform of the biological machine is anything but macrodimensional; in the sleeping state of the human biological machine we feel isolated and apart, but in the waking state, perceiving without the intermediary of machine perceptions, we can see clearly the morphological connectivity, the chain of chambers within which the human biological morphology appears and to which we are connected by identification with this morphology, and we perceive what it is that creates the illusion of life.

We are kept by topological nonconformity from those chambers in which we lack morphological identity, morphological presence. Any given set of morphological structures which we call human will yield roughly sixty-five, seventy, seventy-five, maybe eighty years of total apparent travel-time. We should be able to calculate these morphological contiguities in seconds, or minutes of sequential time, yielding a number which gives us a clearer idea of how much pathway we really have established through the Creation using our present morphological identity.

If we are at all serious about being voyagers, we will want to quickly outgrow the primate morphology which limits us to a single primate lifetime—our present range of total access—in order to gain a wider spectrum of voyaging capability and therefore, a correspondingly greater field of work.

As voyagers we might be willing to take whatever the higher dimensions dish out, but as shamen, in the Work, we must have the discipline not to become caught up in a web of unwanted wandering; we must therefore be able to shapeshift rather fluidly, to alter rapidly our morphology in a way that we are able to access different levels of voyaging . . . .

However, before we are capable of doing anything along these lines, we will have to learn more about ourselves, where we are, where we can and can't go, and where we might be able to go to escape our certain annihilation when our stream of life runs dry, and our present morphology reaches the end of the line.

The essential self is presently limited by identity to the morphology of the human biological machine and cannot expand beyond into domains of the labyrinth where more complex morphologies, typically including what we in our present state would consider environment, atmosphere or other living creatures, are the norm.

The essential self has reached a steady-state association with the human biological machine, having sifted down through the entire spectrum of Creation—much as gold seeps through sand and dirt until it finally comes to rest on bedrock, something of such density that further downward travel is now impossible, and even in bedrock it tends to seek the deepest crevice.

If we are to be of any use in the Work, it is imperative that we move quickly beyond our present primate morphology, embracing new morphologies that will allow us to move more freely throughout the labyrinth, where we will be able to work.

In the ordinary course of events, we come into contact with many morphologies, but because they are composed of familiar morphological constructs—isolated from the greater whole by our own perceptual occlusions, but not separated in fact—they usually go unnoticed unless our attention is drawn to them by some accident or shock, or we have trained ourselves to see them, to draw a more inclusive picture of our world.

Our lives as voyagers begin with work to establish new connectivity and more complex identity-configurations, training our newly expanded attention to follow sensations in the fullest possible intensity, separated from those primate interpretations and visual image-significances normally attached to them, freeing ourselves from the influence of familiar impressions, forming gradually in ourselves a completely new set of interpretative categorical understanding; we could then begin to see the potential for morphological upscale into something entirely different.

Transformations for our work are in general produced in larger circles of voyagers, each of whom has brought to the circle a different typicality; it must be said that these complex invoking clusters, no matter how harmless, inevitably offend one or another tribal or religious taboo somewhere in the primate world.

The art and science of labyrinth voyaging is nowhere more refined than in shamanism; shamanism is not a religion in the modern hysterical-emotional worship—and supplicate—sense; it is an effective method of direct interaction and confrontation with the Absolute.

Shamanism is not for the weak-hearted and has long been feared by the mainstream, rightly so, and equally heartily embraced by the social outcast, not necessarily rightly so. It is this unfortunate association with the cultural outcast that has created the impenetrable wall of superstition which makes it almost impossible to study and practice shamanism in straightforward open simplicity.

Because very few practicing shamen have ever talked or written on the subject, books produced by actual shamen are rare, which makes it almost impossible to study the subject in the written abstract, and many shamen are unrecognized by those not initiated into shamanism, because the signs of shamanism are all but invisible to the non-initiate.

For example, it would surprise most serious scholars to find that the names of Cezanne, Gauguin, Van Gogh, Rembrandt van Rijn, Beethoven, H.G. Wells—whose best and wildest extrapolations, although they reached far beyond the science of the day, such as the hydrogen bomb and air power, still fell very short of the mark because no matter how extravagant the guess, reality surpassed their wildest dreams. Peter Sellers, Einstein, Tesla, Fritz Lang and Gurdjieff—all intuitional invocationists drawing their inspiration down upon them from the macrodimensions, inspiration in the sense of breathing into oneself the intuitional quantum leaps which each of them repeatedly achieved— could conceivably fall under the category of shamanism, if we didn't require other factors of discipline, intent and work-knowledge, while those who followed formula, although famous and admired, such as Monet, Gainsborough, Turner, Edison, Jules Verne—who restricted his science to inventions already existing in patent—Schopenhauer, Mozart, the Beatles—who were more a product of their times than leaders and trendsetters—and Ouspensky, certainly would not.

Nearly the entire organum of written material on shamanism was produced by outsiders who spent a relatively short time with a shaman, and observed shamanism within a highly prejudicial narrow and primitive cultural context and not as a thing-in-itself not unique to tribalism and primitivism. Even favorable prejudice by such observers has been so subjective as to make it no more palatable or fathomable to exocultural study than it ever has been.

Shamanism doesn't seem to belong in any set of axiomatic beliefs which form our contemporary but admittedly incomplete science.

We dislike and tend to disapprove of something which stubbornly delves into phenomena which may suggest glimpses of an expanded world, an entire group of phenomena and meaning existing far beyond the boundaries of our current world-view.

These phenomena are considered inadmissible from the point of view that they contradict the established electro-magnetic and chemical spectrum of accepted scientific mysticism; as anyone in the sciences will freely admit, even the most casual study of historical evidence clearly shows a tendency among established scientists to a status-quo rigidity; what that means is, a fact that doesn't fit is a fact that doesn't exist. This is the kind of cultural poison against which shamanism must continually struggle.

Shamanism is hated and feared for its espousal of temporary truths; for a shaman, each answer suggests a new question, and the unknown is perpetually before us in a never-ending panorama of relativity...an endless, gray landscape of constantly indeterminate values.

The sad fact is that we are all, even the most experienced shamen, involuntary products of the mainstream mentality and its grim consensus reality. Our views and beliefs were programmed into us by the same people who have always been the first to grab the torches and burn down the castle.

We were born to the mob and raised by the mob, and if, for some reason, we don't feel compelled to fall in line, shop at the mall, struggle over unwanted facial hair, zits and armpit odor, wear the latest fashion craze, guzzle bad American beer and scream hysterically and violently at every little baseball, basketball, football, hockey, soccer or badminton score, thrash about and obediently foam at the mouth at every maudlin religious or patriotic assembly, we risk a merciless drawing and quartering before we can make our peace with the god of the primates...the old fella with the long white beard who takes over where Santa Claus leaves off.

Through repeated exposure to the macrodimensions and looking at the world of primates from rather distant climes far outside the human dimension, shamen develop a rather unusual view of primate superstition; social values and beliefs are quickly evaluated as just so much horse-pucky invented strictly for crowd control and economic benefit of the already disgustingly wealthy, and these values are usually turned around one-hundred-and-eighty degrees or completely transcended, making the shaman an unknown quantity, something apart from the culture, someone not to be trusted to follow popular conventions.

For example, the whole subject of spiritism can be approached from a strictly technical, non-mystical point of view. Any competent shaman knows that virtually every phenomenon of spiritism can be produced without ritual or complication just through the correct use of attention.

Attention is a powerful key, a potent invocational tool, because all macrodimensional voyaging is ultimately a function of attention, which is to say, the extension of presence into the total field of potential attention, a concept which has been boiled down many centuries ago into the phrase, "the Kingdom is already at hand".

A shaman learns to concentrate attention, not the attention of the machine, but of the essential self, and even the attention of a whole group in seance, defining the word seance in its simplest meaning, "to sit without doing anything else".

Human primates are easily impressed with unusual phenomena perhaps because they have such powerful self-occlusion, providing little knowledge of themselves and the whole world around them; in the course of ordinary life they have at best only a superficial knowledge of their own human biological machine and none at all about its inner workings and evolutionary potential.

Before we can really be effective labyrinth voyagers, we must first become accurate and attentive observers, including ourselves—even our thoughts and conversation which we take for granted as self-generated and which we assume to be within the grasp of our ordinary attention, but which isn't—in our total field of view.

Even in grade school, we should have learned that when we didn't know the answer to a question, if we paid close attention to it, it would naturally suggest an answer, as a question always will, if we do not wander off into a world of our own in which we hear an imaginary question only vaguely similar to the one actually asked, and then look only to a standard formula for our answers.

The applied use of concentrated attention, if we take our possible intensity of attention as something far beyond the ordinary level of attention which has been for thousands of years sufficient in our society to qualify ourselves among the most intelligent species on the planet, suggests a discipline of attention, but we can see that such a discipline lies far afield from our usual idea, what we ordinarily accept as the power of attention.

With some knowledge of higher dimensional laws, we can construct a resonating chamber in our own dimension and activate it, it will begin to attach itself to a macrodimensional chamber, a receiving resonator, which begins to vibrate in sympathetic unison. This opens a door between dimensional domains and is the most typical form of invocation.

In a sense, we hoist ourselves up by our own bootstraps, developing skills of attention toward self-invocation, of placing ourselves somewhere where we are not.

Our work-attention is only as effective as the attention of the essential self. This special form of attention is the tool to which we will return again and again throughout our lives as voyagers in the labyrinth.

Even if the human biological machine happened to have a functional ordinary attention, machine-attention is of no value in the macrodimensions, and in any case, it doesn't survive well.

If we depend on machine-attention, we are bound to bitter disappointment just shortly following the death of the machine, because everything which the machine has fixated in its attention will also die; everything accomplished by the machine, all its precious self-improvements, will be lost.

It should by now be obvious that magic is strictly a conceptual construct, a convenient way of viewing increased and decreased contact with a segment of the reality spectrum which ordinarily passes unidentified and ignored even in full view.

We can say that "miracles" and "magic" are mere cultural jargon, representing socio-primitive views of various phenomena associated with the intrusion of one dimensional level upon another.

How else can a human primate, immersed in the black-and-white oversimplifications of an education system geared to the lowest common denominator, view superimpositions of one macrodimensional configuration over a lower dimensional configuration?

We have no right to expect a product of the present culture to relate intrusive phenomena resulting from disturbances of morphological correspondence with a new morphological presence which only a moment ago was occluded and now suddenly isn't.

Four hundred years ago, if we suggested that people would fly through the air in big iron birds, that we would be able to see sound, expand our vision, simulate intelligence, capture images and reconstruct them at will on a glass screen, and drive metal monsters at over a hundred miles an hour until a motorcycle policeman stopped us, someone like Leonardo Da Vinci might have agreed with us . . . at least in principle . . . and we might all have burned at the stake together!

And rightly so, because we would have been imposing the realities of another much later temporal configuration upon a world that didn't want them and wasn't ready for them, if it ever is. The primate world is—and always has been—thoroughly rutted, routinized and robotic, and anything which threatens this delicate imbalance is considered uncontrollable and dangerous.

You.
You is.
You is here.
Hi, you.

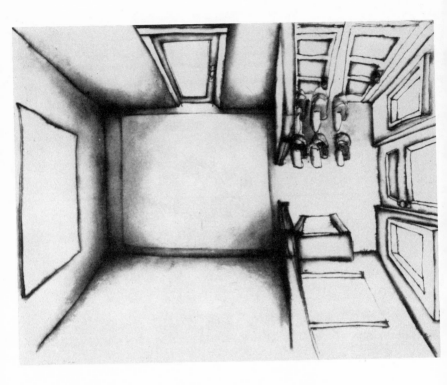

E.J. GOLD, *OVERHEAD PERSPECTIVE OF STUDIO #330,*
PEN & INK WASH, 9''x 12'', 1975.

CHAPTER 10

Data Retrieval
in the Higher Dimensions

Shamanism was first developed thousands of years ago to satisfy macrodimensional needs, something rejected because it is not focused on common primate goals, subject only to higher laws beyond the reach or ken of the human world.

That we may understand the origin of shamanism, we must turn to the ancient world; it was the first form of religion, yet it was not looked upon as a religion; the word "religion" didn't even exist; yet, shamanism today is automatically associated with religion and cultism because human primates can't imagine any use for higher ideas beyond the concept of organised religion.

The appearance of the word "religion" forms a line of demarcation between unembellished macrodimensional voyaging and ritualized pseudo-spiritual hysteria and repression centering around the collection plate, a semi-ornate religious artifact which has its roots in the crushing economic necessities of human civilization.

Shamanism probably appeared at about the same time as the first dim glimmer of intelligence—something we will have to accept for lack of a better word—dawned upon the primates who were to eventually walk erect, stand tall, carry a big stick and proudly refer to their own local tribe as *human beings.*

Exactly eighty thousand, nine hundred and two years ago, the very first shaman, whose name is lost to antiquity, assumed a functional working relationship with the Absolute and also with those macrodimensional beings discovered during the difficult and convoluted ascent and descent up and down the dimensional ladder.

The very first shamen happened by chance to make their discoveries regarding beings and conditions of higher dimensions through their service to the chief of the tribe, for whom they acted as something like modern-day intelligence operatives, conveying themselves—and their macrodimensional information—intact through the dimensional scales, utilizing the *Prometheus Effect* on their village-oriented vision-quests.

A shaman on the tribal level would have been called a medicine chief, responsible for the spiritual well-being of the tribe. Of course, medicine in this sense means much more than just transcendental medication . . . .

So long as it was the battle chief who was in charge of setting the direction and intention of the shaman's vision quests, getting a readout—or the equivalent in the local dialect—on next week's battle was probably highest on the priority list.

Being of accommodating disposition, the shaman would exit from the local dimension, quickly scan the event-horizon for the information he needed, and then bring it back, generally stopping along the way as necessary for furtherance of his shamanic knowledge, equilibrium and higher dimensional stress-management.

Typically a shaman would be debriefed by the tribal council or chiefs and was expected to indicate in dance or song or story what was in The Big Script In The Sky for the following week. He might then suggest a variety of more or less equally hysterical courses which the tribe could take to avoid the highest probability factors for disaster, yet he held himself apart from the outcome.

From his vantage point far above the subjective human dimension, even a tribal shaman should have been able to access material outside the present domain, as John did in Revelations and Nostradamus demonstrated in his quatrains. In effect, he could look ahead in the script to see how things would come out.

If he downscaled directly, he could get himself quite thoroughly mangled unless he happened to have at hand a method of changing morphological form and his sense of identity with morphology rather rapidly; as a result of the rather curtailed life-expectancy of shamen, shapeshifting developed as an art and a skill very quickly, and its elaborations became the foundation for Egyptian mythology, lycanthropy and other forms of shapechanging mythos.

At the very origin of this dangerous profession was the confrontation of various macro-entities utilizing an impressive theatre of feathers, bones and rattles—some of the more colorful paraphernalia associated with earlier primitive forms of shamanism, although we're not above using a few feathers, bones and rattles ourselves even in this sophisticated day and age—to influence the less exalted macrodimensional creatures to at least not work *against* the tribe's welfare and survival which, according to the opinion of most tribes of humans, have always formed the greater part of any macroinhabitant's focus of attention.

Because of this annoying ability to escape the local dimension, to see ahead just a little, and perhaps even pull a few strings, the shaman was always considered extremely strange, yet because he was valuable to the tribe, they didn't lynch him outright.

Because he existed at least partly outside the local dimension, he was not expected to participate seriously in tribal politics and local customs, which is to say, he could be extremely whimsical and yet, due perhaps to the awe and fear in which he was held, remain free of harrassment.

Not surprisingly, the tribe would remain studiedly oblivious to the means by which the shaman accomplished his higher dimensional missions; they didn't know, and they didn't want to know; superstition dictated their occlusion of the specifics of his supernatural connections and powers, in much the same way primate humans tend to avoid contact with the handicapped for fear that it will somehow rub off on them and that the next day they'll wake up crippled...this is, of course, total rubbish; it takes at least six weeks for it to take effect.

Members of the tribe had to accept his many rather amusing and incomprehensible habits, such as periodically bashing his head gently against an odd rock cropping; they laughed at his simple, cunning naïveté, his utter disinterest in participating with them in sudden exciting outbreaks of violence; they found humor in his evident inability to founder as they did in deep fugues of identification with the things they found important, which are to the shaman the more trivial aspects of life.

His tendency to subject himself to severe stress might produce no more than a bewildered shrug, or a questioning glance from his patrons, nor would his use of botanical stimulants, deep emotional religious fugues, artificially induced grand mal seizures, strange music and dance, dangerously prolonged sexual cabal, or incomprehensible contemplative states produce serious reactions in the tribespeople, unless something happened to visibly violate local taboos, as almost anything a shaman does would today, in America.

Even so, a tribe, however civilized, will allow certain violations of its taboos, if the shaman is providing a valuable social service, as is the case with contemporary popular tribal shamen, the rock musician, whose excesses—like the high-roller at a gambling casino who is provided by the outwardly conservative management with virtually anything he desires including exotic drugs and equally exotic prostitutes both male and female—must be overlooked if we are to have any performance at all.

Among early human beings, a shaman was a tribal asset, an egg, metaphorically speaking, to be nurtured and protected; typically he was provided with a warm, dry cave in which to live; food, drugs, implements of all kinds, magical or otherwise; bows and arrows, torches, smudge-pots filled with fine-ground carbon, paint pigments, sculpting tools, clangers, gongs, rattles, drums and other musical instruments; all kinds of herbs and roots and berries; body paints, lamp-fat, women, and anything else he needed to induce the states necessary to upscale into the macrodimensions.

Of course, the elements of tribalism don't disappear just because a tribe makes the transition to an agrarian, industrial or space-age technology, and tribalism is still very much in evidence in our own sophisticated Western civilization, revealing occasionally the same basic operating modes exhibited by slightly less primitive but not quite as barbarous tribes of the past.

Tribal shamanism concerns itself with the business and attitudes of whatever tribal mechanisms are operating: NASA, the Pentagon, and rapidly shifting fashion and fads are part of modern tribal shamanism; for example, the artificial dictates of fashion are imaginary constructs which directly reflect the tribal taboos of the moment. Even the most casual study will clearly reveal, for example, that the real function of fashion is to enhance taboo areas, call them to attention, and make them temporarily attractive, exciting and, more covertly, lucrative.

About seven thousand nine hundred and forty-four years ago, give or take a month, someone powerful whose name has also mercifully been obliterated by time decided to formalize and codify the entire oral tradition, and in accordance with this directive, all existing macrodimensional knowledge was hammered into the Unified Shamanistic Code, the USC, and this was more or less the condition of things by the time of the appearance of the Sumerian shamen.

As far back as the cities and cultures of Ur, Sumer, Elam and Lagash, in the Caspian and Mesopotamian regions—city states which had developed in the Mesopotamian region, between the lower Tigris and Euphrates Rivers and were still operating along tribal lines, although the cultures had become more gregarious and compacted by extreme population density—shamanism had already evolved into something very different from what it had been when the tribes were moveable groups living in temporary encampments; now family lines and business inheritance had assumed the greatest importance.

The Sumerians were surprisingly competent shamen, for all their cultural formalization; actually we should say "shawomen", because until they were murdered by power-hungry priests during the mid-Hellenic period, the majority of practicing shamen were priestesses who had for centuries possessed and used powerful shamanistic methods, almost foolproof induction techniques and incredibly detailed labyrinthine maps with dimensional pathways clearly indicated. A few of their macrodimensional maps survive and are useful even today.

The profound shamanistic knowledge possessed by the Sumerians and Babylonians later formed the main body of classical Sufism; Sufism is usually associated with Islam and believed to originate from it, but Sufism actually predates Islam by several thousand years, as any competent impartial study will reveal.

Sufism is a very elegant form of shamanism generally unrecognized in any but its Islamic form—a social force functioning more or less like Masonic lodges, Lions, Elks, Rotarians, Freemasons, Oddfellows and other business organizations in which the organization exists solely for the sake of the continued existence of the organization.

Some Sufi groups have managed to retain their freedom from the suffocation of Islam, however, and are a veritable hotbed of shamanic activity, primarily in the area of Raimundo Lull's Majorca, the home of Western shamanic alchemy, cabalism, Franciscanism and the *Catalan trouvère*.

As shamanism developed from a formal science into a broad, intuitive art, the inevitable separation into two main branches became more and more accentuated. On the one hand, tribal shamanism served the purpose of the tribe, and, on the other hand, a hidden and unknown form of shamanism, passed from generation to generation from initiate to initiate in carefully closed societies, served the secret purposes of work among the beings of the macrodimensions.

The Babylonians, Sumerians and Mayans developed fabulously innovative and elaborate techniques of shape-shifting through some of the most extravagantly exotic macrodimensional morphology anyone ever encountered along the totemic ladder.

They had a remedy for just about everything, including those excruciating, breathless suspensions at the dreaded wavelength fundamentals—a fundamental being defined as the root-tone of a harmonic series, which is to say, a component having the lowest frequency in a complex vibration—where the shamen would be forced to stop momentarily to gather the wherewithal necessary to bridge the gap of sudden energy retardation.

The shapeshifting developed by these early voyagers helps us today to reduce the shock of transition and make intermediate passages much more gentle, enabling many more shamen to live to a ripe old age. From then on, shapeshifting became an integral part of shamanism, just as it is today.

By the time the city of Sumer had fully developed and was ripe and ready for self-destruction, these early city dwellers had a very highly evolved, exotic and sophisti-cated—in the best sense of the word, not in its present meaning of unnecessary complication—form of shamanism which had sprung from a hunting and killing society's preoccupation with game, water, health, wealth, safety, fertility, fecundity and longevity.

The Sumerian shaman found himself moving into a new form of shamanism in which he or she was expected to operate in very specific formalized ways to contact very specific macrodimensional beings in the religious pantheon of the local homo sapiens; these activities were rather fully documented in little interdimensional travelogs which have come down to us today in a highly bastardized form, the Medieval versions of which compose the body of work under the category of grimoire.

What actually went on in the back rooms of temples in ancient civilizations such as Sumer, Ur and Nimrud we can understand only if we are able to stand in the sandals of the people who lived in the dawn of history; but even though we know little about how they lived and worked in their daily lives, they left us a pictorial legacy of their shamanic shapeshifting techniques, how they used the side-step dance of morphological change, represented as animal forms but probably exactly the same expansions as we use today, to plow through the more vicious domains of the higher dimensions.

Some of the Sumerian shamen ended up as enslaved teachers to the Babylonians, Syrians, Chaldeans, and other aggressive Mesopotamian tribes. They also ended up in other places; the Sumerians opened colonies to the East, notably at Mohenjo-Daro, and as far Northwest as Britain and Ireland, which exhibit a few pieces of archaeological evidence of brief occupation. And why not, the Romans and Phoenicians did the same much later.

Shamanism became progressively more structured, more formalized, and found its way into Egypt, influencing profoundly the founding of Mosaic Judaism by Moses, an Israeli living as a royal Egyptian during the period of the Captivity.

Sumerian-Babylonian tribal shamanism flourished during the Ramses period. At about the same time, a group of practitioners developed a profession which dealt with instructions to the dead: how to pass through the corridors of the underworld and the world of the dead, another form of labyrinth voyage.

The science of guiding the dead through the underworld was passed on from father to son; it was a family business. Practitioners would paint instructions for movement through the afterlife onto the wall of the tomb. This was perpetuated through various texts.

The Papyrus of Ani illustrates one lineage of such pictographic instruction supported by hieroglyphic text which eventually found its way into Western civilization and re-emerged in such later forms as *The Necronomicon* in which we find more than just a simple straightline revamping of the Middle Kingdom instructions for passing through the various portals, chambers, and corridors in the higher dimension.

This is all a very exact business that has historically been jealously guarded, nobody is quite sure by whom. The practitioners who could actually be considered members of a specialized branch of non-recreational voyaging shamen tended to use the same basic techniques that shamen had been using ever since the Absolute made that first big mistake we've spent our whole existences living down, entropically speaking.

To perform macrodimensional operations successfully, shamen required a *totem,* a vertical series of pyramidic forms—largest singular at the top, smallest but most numerous at the bottom—through which they were able to shapeshift their way up and down, sometimes managing to avoid utter self-destruction and general mayhem in the course of their voyage; sometimes the totem was represented in the form of a carved stick or pole, a series of paintings or petroglyphs, or a string of beads, which served as a reminder of the totality of possible shapeshifting morphologies available to the shaman, who might become lost in the voyage so much so that he could forget his place on the macrodimensional map.

These early experimenters discovered something important about assuming the shapes of animals—meaning their characteristics and attributes—which later formed the basis for the dynastic and protodynastic Egyptian shamanism; the attributes of certain animals helped them to extend their morphology far beyond the human primate form; we should understand that the idea is not to assume the actual shapes of these animals, but that animal shapes could be used to *suggest* how the human morphology might be extended.

Instructional texts like *The Papyrus of Ani* recommended specific totemic form expansions for each macrodimensional chamber, represented as the afterlife, and to the practicing shaman, these animalistic symbols had very different meanings than their modern archaeo-anthropo-logical interpretation would lead one to believe . . . .

They were familiar with animals in ways that we are not, and used them to draw upon the characteristics of higher dimensional beings; animal forms were used as a notation system to guide voyagers into the recognition of chambers and their higher dimensional inhabitants. This corresponds roughly to the birdlike attributes of the characters in Attar's *Conference of the Birds*.

Shapeshifting is a means by which the shaman is able to voyage up and down the full spectrum of dimensional scales without totally disastrous consequences and without getting himself obliterated beyond recall. Shapeshifting takes place during the periodic retardations on the vertical macro-dimensional axis, represented as figures on an ascending and descending scale.

Although voyaging shamen couldn't actually be permanently destroyed—which is part of their ongoing problem as well as their guarantee of continuation in the Work — their information and knowledge could become distorted or obliterated, and they could be temporarily destroyed, which is just slightly worse than finding half a worm in your apple.

Totems used for shapeshifting were originally hollow columns of descending forms inside which the shamanic voyager would climb up and down, such as those used by the Mayans in their religious ceremonies.

Rituals were enacted to draw down a higher entity through the totem or column, which became a lightning rod for the descending form to surround the totemized shaman.

The shaman would then leave the totem, communi-cate the macrodimensional data, and through him or her the macrodimensional inhabitant would demonstrate its job in the real world.

Initiates could ask questions of the entity, but this

required exact knowledge and an understanding of macrodimensional language; they had to know how to extract reliable information without offending it—macrodimensional entities tend to be very short-tempered, during their hopefully brief encounter with lesser species.

By divination, the shaman would try to get an indication as to which entity was angry with the tribe, or which entity turned its back on the tribe. Then he would set out to visit that entity in its own dimension and its own chamber, and doing so, he would select a partner or several partners who as a whole, acting and arousing a subjective state with him in concert, best represented that entity as a sum of all its parts. This still remains true today of all shamanistic practices.

The shaman may use miniature morphological apparati, on the principle that the model of the thing *is the thing itself*, and that the more exact the model, the more similar and archetypal the model becomes, the more readily it provides the shaman access into a higher or lower dimension—this ladder, now known as Jacob's Ladder or the Golden Ladder of Magdelene, enables the shaman to move up and down the scale.

A shaman sometime between the dawn and midafternoon of human civilization would have undergone a certain degree of self-discipline, but there were no schools of shamanism and the skills were passed on orally and practically from one generation to the next.

Any unusual discipline was largely physical, along the lines of the Eastern Asian fakir; mental and emotional disciplines were already an important part of tribal life, while the radical absence in contemporary civilization of such mental and emotional disciplines requires that they be artificially reintroduced in anyone who aspires to modern professional shamanism.

Up until the mafia-inspired drug laws of the nineteen-thirties, nobody thought anything of taking a vegetrate substance, a little assisting factor—mushroom, herb or plant—either ingesting it or inhaling the smoke, since that was the quickest and surest way to induce the states and the visions sought after, until the relatively recent invention, about four hundred and twenty five B.C., of self-induced grand mal seizures and emotional-hysterical trance states which became very popular in their more modern version, circa the 1920's, in rare mediumistic style.

Today's shaman has a powerful array of drug-free methods of induction, and can operate independently of the need for vegetable substances; mental-emotional techniques have been developed and disseminated over a wide area of the world, and induction methods which were once restricted to blood-sworn members of intensely secret societies are now available in paperback.

Aside from the more popular Twentieth Century tribal figures, the Blue Giant rock stars, Red Giant movie stars, White Dwarf baseball stars, and political shooting stars, to name a few of the more obvious local stellar phenomena, tribal shamanism has degenerated into an astronomically formalized cult, devoid of any true macrodimensional knowledge; real shamanism has become something totally feared and anathema to modern day human primates, despite what certain "trends" might lead us to believe.

Today, shamen of the Work lineage are not so well received by their contemporaries; more often than anyone would care to acknowledge, one comes along and upsets the complacent apathy of the establishment. Nothing stops a shaman from appearing within any kind of system, because he can use any set of circumstances, which is what shamanic shapeshifting is all about.

When a non-tribal, macrodimensionally oriented shaman comes along, shock waves spread like wildfire; in the skillful but socially merciless hands of a non-tribal shaman, any harmless custom or belief can suddenly become the most explosive device imaginable!

The shaman takes unexpected turns, and what makes the mainstream squirm is that he uses very familiar objects, but in very unfamiliar ways, upsetting anyone in whom the belief has been inculcated that we ought to allow only one use for each item, maintaining the thoroughly flat view of an artificially simplified world.

The serious shaman is destined to a life of more or less permanent exile from the masses, isolated forever from the most common denominator; yet, even from this lonely existence, he has little disposition toward climbing back into the mainstream of life; the expectations and goals that stem from the human realm are no longer part of his makeup, if they ever had been; the shaman's vision remains sharply focused on the needs of macrodimensional life. All shamanic actions stem from this total devotion to the higher, which offers a life and a set of values considerably different from the social and biological imperatives of lower dimensions.

Real, non-tribal shamanism represents true knowledge, opposed but not aggressively or militarily so, to the ignorance of organized religion, serving the necessities which originate in the highest dimension of the Absolute, following the descending order of turtles, turtles, turtles, all the way down.

From any ordinary human primate's point of view—which simply reflects the prevalent beliefs and customs of any age—the shaman follows utterly and completely incomprehensible, disturbing and unknown natural laws which don't even exist in, or correspond to, any known principles of common popular science.

A shaman's unwavering devotion to a single, pure aim with unflinching integrity may appear, to someone acting under the laws of ever-changing nature, highly illogical and disjointed from the viewpoint of change as linear reality; in addition, the shaman's curiously disinterested view of human primate pursuits can be terrifyingly incomprehensible.

The shaman borrows the form of whatever culture or belief system he happens to find himself in, and promptly proceeds to violate the cultural conventions by using each of these elements as an invocational instrument, disassembling and reassembling it—and himself in relation to the element—and from then on he is called a heretic, until shortly after his demise, when those who vilified him begin typically to worship him and embalm his memory; within a few generations we find that he has been permanently ensconced as the patron saint of some craft guild or other, and everything he ever produced is debriefed, reworked into an acceptable form, scrubbed and whitewashed of any embarrassments and marketed shamelessly to the surviving generations.

The shaman, however strange to the ordinary he may appear, is perfectly normal within the context of shamanism. What he does and how he does it is completely and unquestionably self-evident, his directives and imperatives far removed from mainstream ideas and values, outrageously provocative and scandalous from the primate view; to be sure, he need make no special effort to guarantee an angry fear-reaction in his mainstream contemporaries.

Unfortunately for anyone's peace of mind, especially his own, a shaman's behavior will tend to be a blend of his most annoying manifestations, magnifying his complex conflictual relationship with social protocol; nerve-wracking non-sequitur and unexpected blasphemies constantly send ripples of shock waves through unsuspecting bystanders; he seems utterly unresponsive to the most obsequious blandishments . . . .

Even an apparently simple thing like a common language which we are all forced to use in order to communicate with others becomes something different in the hands of a shaman. Shamen always seem to lean heavily toward those tooth-gnashing, fingernail-scraping, annoyingly Ivesian-Stravinskian-Schoenbergian ways of communicating that just don't seem to be able to conform themselves to well-defined human conventions.

A shaman will tend to use non-verbal but eminently communicable types of exchange, a sort of ineffable spiritual grimace which best expresses his overall attitude toward primate life in general.

His outlook is based partly on the knowledge that words have a definite disaster potential in higher spaces, that words confine the spirit; his boundless being strives to escape the narrow confines of definitions, descriptions, and mental judgments which arise from the mind.

A shaman will often seem to make a sudden shift toward left field, leaving the linear literal mind holding the bag, so to speak, temporarily off-balance and unsure of its footing, but the shaman knows that nothing is ambiguous; he sees the underlying causes and knows how to attune himself to them. He knows the irony of expectation, and the ecstasy of disappointment; he has learned to follow life as one's vision follows the face of a lover.

The shaman seldom becomes known in this world and, as he tames his first, wild, exuberant shamanism, he becomes even more invisible.

Under ordinary circumstances, those who come directly into contact with a very great shaman tend to renounce him, but organize a church which springs inevitably from his teaching. A real shaman may allow a lineage to appear briefly, knowing that it will vanish into the murky mist of religion, absorbed and transmogrified into cultural invisibility.

The duration of the necessity for the existence of a school will vary, its necessity unconnected to any single, married, separated, divorced or temporarily involved individual but rather to a specific set of circumstances existing on a higher dimension.

The life of a school is always circumscribed; schools are not meant to exist indefinitely because they fulfill specific purposes. Schools exist when there is a need for Work. This reflects the greater relation of the Work to the Creation. The Work is not something stable and repetitive; it changes constantly, and it has many forms.

Though the availability of the Work may fluctuate, and its form may change radically, the nature of the Work never changes, though many neophyte shamen may fall into the trap of convention, devoting their entire work-lives to the dead forms of the past.

When a school has died before the completion of a task, another school appears to finish the business of the first.

**A man's work ends
At the setting sun;
A shaman's work
Is never done.**

E.J. GOLD, *COSMO STREET HALLWAY,*
PEN & INK WASH, 12''x9'', 1975.

CHAPTER 11

Shapeshifting up the Totem

Voyaging back and forth between the human and other dimensions, using powerful mental and emotional equations to produce a tangible construct, a totemic ladder, a dimensional elevator, the voyager shapeshifts through the totemic morphologies up, down, or both at once.

That we may perform our obligation-tasks in the macrodimensions, we must learn to move freely in unobstructed pathways through space, and this freedom of movement depends almost wholly upon the use of a combination of whole body habitude in general and the mask for further definition; the mask is a simple name for a complex network-construct of identity, posture, form, sound, scent, and all of the elements which constitute a living morphological boundaried sense of self, existing temporarily—always temporarily—somewhere in the Great Labyrinth which we call the Creation.

The mystery of the mask; a thin layer of self-reality held in place by the hand, as a lorgnette; color and form worn across the face, produced by grimace, supported and uplifted by vocal distortion, extensions of the diaphragm, lungs, expansions and contractions of the whole body attention; a subtle assumption of postures, gestures, moods, and forms of macrodimensional characters, topological trickery enabling the shaman to assume the viewpoint, to thoroughly and microscopically examine the new state and sense of self gained through ecstatic expansion of the morphological identity.

Mystery of masks? No mystery; the shaman uses the mask in much the same way that Londoners might take the underground, Moscovites the tube, New Yorkers the subway, Parisians the Metro, Disneylanders the skyway, and Catholic priests the breviary.

A shaman may have a thousand or ten thousand masks, but because he grasps the foundation, the principles by which many more may be constructed, he may find and use anything at hand.

Costume, music, lighting, sounds taken from the atmosphere or made from the mouth, hands, feet, hair, fingertips, armpits or pelvis orchestrate the emotional fugue, interwoven improvisational movement piercing the silence of the invocational studio, a quiet walk on a busy street, a fiery dance before an audience of one.

Trans-dimensional force, flying on the heels of concentrated attention, compounding itself in definite gradations of primary intensity, is what we call the First Water, the *dosage-d'eau*.

The movements, sounds, sights and smells; the masks and costumes, postures, and atmospheric ambience; the comprehensive view of the environment; all this comprises the left-hemisphere world view, what we may call *à la monde gauche*.

The mental and emotional structure, the state of the shaman, especially the sense of identity carried into the work-studio, we could term *promenade homme*, meaning the totality of mental-emotional mood of the shaman before the invocation begins.

All these taken together form the invocational trinity, *dosage d'eau, à la monde gauche,* and *promenade homme*, which translated to common English would give us the concepts of set, setting and dosage.

As experienced macrodimensional day-commuters, we are quite aware that in order to voyage from one point to another, we must inevitably pass through several stations, each mask a Station of the Way.

To extemporaneously voyage and navigate without the convenience of props and costume whenever the need arises, makeshift and improvisation are the voyager's stock in trade.

The instinct for navigation is omnipresent; to the macro-mind that made the labyrinth, the apprehension of the chaotic form is as natural as our instant appreciation of a symphony, but only as a totality; to the shaman, chaos—the spectrum of reality outside the realm of imposed order—is as readable as a roadmap.

Unlike the human primate, that champion of the superficial, the shaman takes whatever time and trouble necessary to discover the keys that open the way; profound powers of concentrated attention establish connections between primate-centered events and vast domains of networked macrochambers.

The lightning path is that which thrusts us into the Work the quickest, not that which serves our subjective aims; we can use our voyaging to escape the confining gravitational attraction of biological mediocrity, placing ourselves dangerously in a position where we can be of real service to the Work, while we still have some blood left to give.

Shamanism is the fastest, most ego-disintegrating and emotionally explosive of all the ways; it brings us directly and wholly into the Work, now and forever, long before we feel really ready to tackle the job.

The shaman must take risks, some quite serious; in this high-risk occupation the survival rate is not too high; those who happen to survive do so by sheer chance, and then they're around for a very long time after; those who don't, tend not to last very long in any case. The casualty rate is high, but we can rest easy; the truly deadly mistakes are all fatal; the quivering cadaver tells the tale.

The shaman never experiments just for the sake of experimentation because of boredom, restlessness or a need for a new brand of excitement—unless it's absolutely convenient.

The fact is, shamen may be anxious, agitated, dazed and confused, but never bored, restless or in need of excitement. A bored shaman is a dead shaman. In the Heart of the Labyrinth, primate imperatives are the ticket to certain destruction.

Shamanism is a business in the same sense that any other form of work is a business and, just like any other business, is forced to operate on profit margin which in turn depends upon cost-efficiency.

Voyaging through the labyrinth, not unlike shopping the mall, has its own price to pay, nothing more, certainly, than the hungriest and most extravagant designer-label buyer—you know the kind, the ones with the T-shirt that says, **I shop, therefore I am**—is willing to pay; no, that's not true . . . actually, the price is much higher than any designer-label buyer would be willing to pay . . . .

Well, then, any shaman worth his weight in metallic salts will, if he values his work, ascertain that the results of labyrinthine voyages are worth the inevitable heavy extortion, or he or she won't be able to repeat the experiment for very long.

The shaman is therefore forced to use the most ruthlessly efficient means to accomplish shamanistic purposes, as long as it doesn't cause harm, and quickly learns that personal profit cannot be taken from the general fund.

Above all, the experienced shaman is aware of the terrible cost of recreational voyaging, and is convinced, sometimes at great personal expense, of the need for voyaging honorably, maintaining an unshakable, but not unnecessarily grim, integrity of purpose.

In all honesty, one must admit that there is no choice; no choice in the sense that if we are able to feel responsible, even if we aren't, and happen to envisage some spilt milk on the floor, we'll sponge it up, *because somebody has to do it.*

A labyrinth-wise voyager needs no better reason; we know that should we choose not to clean it up, no punishment, no blame, no harm; the milk will simply remain, dry up and harden, and sooner or later, when we come back this way again, we'll find it just a little more difficult to clean, but unfortunately, never entirely impossible.

We always have the option of not entering the maze and not performing the Work; no shame in letting the cup pass; in any case, we have no guarantee that we'll actually be able to perform the Work, even if we wish to and find ourselves in a position to... Most of us who set out on the path will never even get a foot hoisted, but this shouldn't discourage us from taking an introductory workshop or two. There's no limit to the number who can *serve* the Work, and the need for cannon fodder—inexperienced and expendable troops—is always endless... you know, like the orange-uniformed Star-Trek studio-contract actors who beam down to their certain death along with the unkillable quintet: Kirk, Spock, McCoy, Chekov and Sulu; you see one of those one-size-fits-all orange uniforms, you know... you just *know* ... they're going to die.

The objective fate of those who do not enter the Work is no worse than the fate of those orange-uniformed security troopers and, in a sense, the fate of those of us who got ourselves engulfed, swallowed and absorbed into the Work is much worse because, by choosing to remain in the Work, among the never-resting, we have chosen the path of no return, a never-ending fate far worse than death, and it is this aspect which is most forbidding to the neophyte.

A shaman will never forget the higher purposes of the essential self in spite of the pressures of the biological machine which, like all other biological machines, could not, in all fairness, be said to share, exactly, in the voyager's boundless enthusiasm for the Work, although it will have served us well if only it brings the essential self into a position of transformation and evolution, providing us with the post-human potential to work in the Work and not just for the Work or—even worse—for ourselves.

Shamanism is not totemism, but it depends upon the totem for its methods of vertical and lateral movement; relatively primitive in its beginnings, in the sense that it was tribally oriented, the content and techniques of shamanism have never been primitive, and are probably less so now than ever before.

Totemism, as it stands today, is not a primitive form of religion that uses animal spirits in its repertory of supernatural deities, nor is it some kind of magical hocus-pocus.

Totemism is founded on the basic understanding that all identities both manifest and unmanifest, can be understood as totemic forms—isolated and distinct morphological configurations which are, through expansion, transcendable—existing simultaneously and correspondingly in many dimensions at once, their unique cross-dimensional point-to-point similarity providing the potential for assumption by total but temporary identity in the mathematically rational sense.

The totemic column appears smaller at the bottom, in the lower dimensions, and overwhelmingly, almost unbearably, vast in the macrodimensional capital, but in proper perspective, from broadside, it looks more like Kwakiutl masks carved into one of those massive British Columbian telephone poles.

The descent to Earth through a lightning rod portrays changes in totem polarity, the descent of archetypal beings leading us eventually into the lower dimensions.

Being traditionally human, we find ourselves irritatingly familiar with a definite set of morphological configurations; a self-imaged view of our own apparently permanent and unchangeable identity which determines what is our lifelong niche somewhere in the totem, and restricts our ability to voyage much beyond the primate level.

When we occupy a chamber and are at home in it, we need not remain for long before we make a place for ourselves there forever.

The art of evaluating our position, discovering exactly which level of totem we happen to be sitting in at the moment, should not occupy a place of mystery; it's actually no more difficult to learn than medical or psychological diagnosis, and we can be assured of a profound surfeit of locational clues in any given chamber.

If we are to work at different dimensional levels, then we must have formal presence in more than one domain, and have the psychological tolerance and control over the concentrated diffusion of our attention to achieve the morphological expansion necessary to penetrate several levels on many widely varying octaves across the total dimensional spectrum.

Our expanded morphological identities—as voyagers, we will have far more than just the one with which human primates are equipped—provide us with a natural connection to macrodimensional bodies.

If we had the vision to share in the macrodimensional life, then we would see and comprehend from within the trans-dimensional characteristics of the essential self, the voyager; but until we are able to achieve this vision, a large part of our own essential nature eludes us and therefore, we cannot say that we really know ourselves beyond the level of the primate machine.

The *Papyrus of Ani* depicts the labyrinth as a series of chambers, each intrinsically containing exact instructions for vertical and lateral movement by shapeshifting. The *Papyrus* is only one such map for professional shapeshifters, which tells us, *now the morphology of a snake, now the general form of a coyote, now a wolf.*

These instructions carry the same intent as the Bardic songs memorized by the Druids in their strictly oral tradition:

"I have been a drop in the air.
I have been a shining star.
I have been a word in a book.
I have been a book in the First Place.
I have been a light in a lamp . . .
A year and a day . . .

I have been a sword in the hand.
I have been a shield in the fight.
I have been the string of a harp,
Spellbound to the cycle of a twelvemonth
In the tidal froth.
I have been a faggot in the fire.
I have been an oak in a grove.
There is nothing
Which I have not been."

Moving into a chamber, we borrow a morphological identity, and according to this idea, we can only go where we already exist; this takes into account all subtleties pervading exact and approximate correspondings.

For example, in certain very remote chambers we might realize, with a little dismay, that there are no forms which even remotely resemble our own morphology and so, if we wish to penetrate such a chamber we will be forced to extend our morphology into a correspondingly accommodating morphological form within the macrochamber.

In the course of our macrodimensional voyaging, we may note with some amusement a considerable latitude between our ordinary human and macrodimensional morphologies.

For example, in the human dimension we might begin as four human primates sitting around a table having dinner, and then, suddenly, as we enter the next higher dimension we might come to realize that morphologically speaking, we are now four large overly communicative cockroaches sitting around a large late Directoire lump of charcoal and, although our expansion into macrodimensional forms is eminently visible from an outside vantage point, we could have easily missed the change, because the momentum of our habitual subjective view confines us to our customary representation of ourselves in the form we have come to recognize as our own; we expect to remain as we are and have always been, and therefore do not recognize it when we happen to escape our customary morphology, even intentionally in the course of macrodimensional voyaging, unless we remember to be aware of these alterations in morphology and have learned to see beyond our automatic transference of imagery from the shockingly bizarre into the all-too-familiar.

In the primate state, the reverberations of which tend to carry over in the higher dimensions in spite of all precautions to the contrary, we lack the equipment to detect the subtle morphological change unless we also happen to notice a radical macrodimensional change, which is so rare as to offer no hope of expanding our vision just by accident.

In music, the exponential nature of expansion is shown by the frequency relationships between the center-scale note and the same note an octave higher, so that a'— a prime — has a frequency of 440hz, a''—a prime-prime — an octave higher, has a frequency of 880hz, a'''—a prime-prime-prime — an octave higher still, has a frequency of 1760hz, and so on.

Intervals within the octave, which can be defined as progressive retardations of wavelength periodically partially destroyed by wave-interference and reciprocal absorption, are governed entirely by mathematical relationships which develop from relatively simple fractional relationships such as 3/2 for the very consonant interval of the perfect fifth, to much more complex fractions for highly dissonant intervals such as the minor second and major seventh.

The laws of macrodimensional voyaging can, with a heavy mallet and a little silicon, be made to correspond to musical notation but, as any macrodimensional being will tell you, the mathematics of music are safest when cloistered in the abstract.

It is interesting to note that retardations — taken as predictably periodic relaxations of energy-exchange — do not follow a strict progression from octave to octave. This becomes particularly evident in music when *just intonation* — a system of tuning in which the true, exact interval relationships in a given key are maintained during the tuning procedure — is employed.

When a composition in one key is played using just intonation, even an untrained listener can determine that the sounds seem unusually rich, full and resonant. However, should a modulation, changing tonality from one tonal center or key to another, be made to a foreign key – a tonal center with a difference of more than two accidentals in the key signature — spectacular dissonances will render the listener almost helpless; the retardations in the new key will give the impression that the world has just tilted thirty-seven and a half degrees.

Just intonation allows no adjustment for the naturally occurring retardation within the octave, and while this results in a greater apparent in-tuneness within a given key or tonal center, the cumulative error to intervals in other tonal centers results in these centers being functionally unusable.

By contrast, in equal temperament, a small artificial adjustment is made to every interval — no one interval is as correctly in tune as with just intonation, and the truth is lost in the process, but modulation from any one key to any other key is more or less equally possible without serious loss.

Musical notation has been used in the past to predict astronomical events, the results of which were, as we would expect, overthrown as instrumentation demonstrated the failure of musical notative structure to uphold itself from the abstract to the applied science.

However, the developing awareness of the consequences of retardation in terms of the octave in astronomy and music of the Sixteenth, Seventeenth and early Eighteenth Centuries is a curious history of intuition and rapidly accelerating instrument accuracy.

The great astronomer, Copernicus, working in the Fifteenth Century made major errors in his astronomical calculations, stemming from the fact that he was working with a mathematically regular progression without accounting for the retardation, the gap. In music of this era, just intonation was predominant.

In the Seventeenth Century, Kepler worked with the laws of music in his astronomical theories. In the early Eighteenth Century, the composer Bach worked with the laws of mathematics in his musical compositions. Both were among the first to successfully acknowledge this irregularity or retardation — Kepler through his theories corrected many misconceptions left by Copernicus, and Bach through his masterful compositions, demonstrated his whole-hearted espousal of the understanding of equal temperament as a universal tuning system.

So the totem is "just", which is to say, true intonation, and the relationship between forms exponential. Levitation, invisibility and the control of someone else's love-life aside, real power is an exponential increase of being, the ability to increase our morphological presence in greater and still greater topological domains.

The totem: an instructional device for professional shapeshifters, initiates who must know thousands of difficult morphologies.

Practicing the totem, we upscale on our own initiation, pull ourselves up by our own bootstraps, get a leg up without a groom to hold the ladder, observation and deduction our only allies; we can find help one figure at a time, each helping step an antiphony responding to our momentum; we must take a step on our own before we can expect a helping response.

The key to macrodimensional movement: we never know where we are going, nor the deeper meaning of what we are doing, but we always can know where we are.

Extending our morphological identity into greater and more complex topological domains we must solve the riddle of the present chamber, allowing us an easy penetration into deeper domains.

Beginning our career as professional shape-shifters, we come to understand each morphology along the totem, each being-obligation-task, as if we were to register with an employment agency. "They", whomever "they" is—we only know that they is not us and that we is not them—look us over, after which we can rightly choose only from those jobs for which we are really qualified—due perhaps to the course of our lives and the resulting effects of cultural conditioning upon the machine which can only transform as it is enabled... Perhaps three or four possible positions will already be filled, leaving us little actual choice.

With our chosen totem, we practice ascension and descent up and down Jacob's Ladder from the assumption of the Empty Throne, the highest form in which we become the ultimate absence, into the depths of the mineral world.

We discipline ourselves to the task, to voluntary slavery; voluntary because although we can let the cup pass from our hands at any moment, we choose to drink from the cup of life, letting the peace of death pass us by.

We love life; we do not reject it with occlusion; this is the secret of our extreme presence; we accept our place in the world, and seek no refuge in sleep.

An enormous mansion; many chambers... we see before us six doors; choosing one, we pass through into the next chamber, within which we see another ten doors, and again we must choose a portal to continue our penetration.

We must have courage to assume the expanded morphological forms necessary for macrodimensional movement, and the non-artificial, which is to automatically imply non-human, intelligence to follow with exactitude the path suggested by intuitional labyrinthine clues.

It is for our intuition that we need our Ariadne, the female spirit of the labyrinth; we will find her within us as we realize our feminine nature and learn that we can trust her implicitly to provide us with beneficent, but not always clear, guidance. In this sense, clarity depends entirely on our willingness to focus the attention, and to keep it from being swept downstream in the bubbling, rushing rapids of the mind.

When a shaman wants
To land on the sun
He's no fool,
He goes
At night.

CHAPTER 12

Encounter with the Simurgh: A School Experiment

In the course of several centuries, it is only rarely that a large group of individuals may be able to openly organize penetrations into macrodimensions and explorations of sectors of the labyrinth ordinarily inaccessible to individuals or smaller groups.

By coincidence or design, thirty had gathered that night for what was to have been an ordinary meeting.

It was announced that an invocational experiment was to take place, using a private performance of *The Creation Story Verbatim*, a full-length play with two characters, The Lord and Archangel Gabriel.

For several days prior to the actual experiment the work group had endured intense invocational voyaging together.

A strange blending of incenses issued from a censer as a thick white candle slowly gave up its waxen life.

The cloud of incense settled gradually and the atmosphere in the chamber thickened. A murky, ominous gloom descended upon us.

A scale model of Cosmo Street—the earliest location of the school known to us, where many mysterious labyrinthine macrodimensional voyages had been said to have occurred—was brought in and placed ceremoniously beside the incense and candle.

Persian carpets of different colors and patterns had been carefully laid out on the floor, providing a rich and lavish setting.

Shoes were left by the entrance to the chamber, and students avoided altogether walking on the carpets. As our vision adjusted itself throughout the course of the evening, the carpets became a swirling, dangerous pool, an electric liquid.

The chamber had been thoroughly cleaned that afternoon, and the Angelic Embassy flags placed on a low table to the left of the stage on which the actors were to recite the play.

Beside the stage lay a chest made of rosewood, ebony and Egyptian mahogany, representing the Ark of the Covenant. Across the room, pulsating and glowing, stood the model of Cosmo Street.

The experiment began at nine o'clock. Seating arrangement was random at first, but then, immediately prior to the performance, we were carefully reseated in specific places and even arranged in sub-groups.

The Lord was seated on the floor up against large comfortable cushions. Gabriel was standing and moving around considerably—nervously trying to lock down his approach and find the right tone. His acting was energetic. There were several starts and stops, backtrackings and switchings.

The actors explored various postures and pitch, groping for the correct mood and intonation, and on several occasions asked for audience feedback.

The intention was to keep the acting at a minimum and, if possible, eliminate it altogether.

They sat face to face, on chairs placed between the two large banco windows on the outer wall of the adobe style living room which served as our theatre, and began afresh.

From that moment on, things began to happen.

Everything artificial and theatrical had been stripped away from the performance, leaving the dialogue intact with its own inner power; the performance had never been so funny, so wild; laughter rippled and broke in waves, yet they never acted.

Almost imperceptibly the atmosphere darkened; it was the same, and yet somehow, indefinably different. The play slowly crawled into life, its macrodimensionality progressively revealing itself.

It became obvious that this was one of those spaces which encapsulates and isolates itself, for which there can be no outside observers. We knew that this would become another of those incommunicable experiences with which we exhaust ourselves in fruitless attempts to share its richness and depth of meaning, succeeding only in reducing it to a thin, meaningless shell....

Voyaging through the labyrinth; this time it wasn't theory, it was real, it was happening, and it was happening to *us*.

Other than the directives "don't act" and "gather and place your unbroken attention on the actors", no guidelines were offered; no direction suggested. Only later were we able to discuss, progressively see and understand the vivid spectrum of impressions, sensations, feelings, and views which we had unknowingly shared.

The actress who played the Lord at one point felt as if her breath alternately filled and then evacuated the environment, and it was noticeable to us all that as she breathed, the entire surrounding circle breathed with her.

This first subtle shift gave the first indication that dimensional crossover had taken place; the first level of macrodimensional attention had been attained, heralded by sensations, and then perceptions, completely and very uncomfortably outside the customary human primate domain.

The breathing stabilized; a deliberate group inhalation followed by rapid exhalation. Something was being pumped up, expanding... a definite presence of something that hadn't been there before, and now it was.

We were aware of each other's deep and slowly growing apprehension, yet there was something that wanted to look at it, and at the same time a fear of looking directly at it, perhaps with the knowledge that the trauma would force us to downscale.

The image of feathers, blue and green; feathers connected to something very large. A bird...a peacock... breathing....

Images flashed in rapid disjointed order, leaving us puzzled, questioning, wondering....

A rustle here, there, an arpeggio of rippling movement culminating in a crescendo of rattling, settling; the only sound like that would be a peacock in full display. That was when we all looked in the direction of the sound.

The thing settled in; we breathed; it puffed.

Most vivid was the final rustling and fan-spread; an indelible image that none of us would ever forget.

From where we were sitting, it seemed to settle into the hallway, then back to the rear of the building, sweeping clockwise around the periphery of the chamber until it reached the area near the hallway leading to the kitchen. There it swept back in the other direction.

One striking impression, a sense of something that had to do with the size of the creature. It felt *huge,* utterly immense.

The very *creature-ness* of this thing left the most vivid memory of all, an unparadoxical intimate majesty; its sheer *livingness* was overwhelming.

A fluctuation; at once we were voyaging in the labyrinth, then, suddenly, hosting a macrocreature, the actors forming the apex, then the body, then the audience plus actors forming the body.

We understood that the actors were playing to only *one*; that the audience itself was one single entity, a combined form and consciousness which, for the moment, regarded the play with a burning intensity of concentration.

It wasn't a play, not in the way we ordinarily understand—an amusing bit of entertainment, something to occupy an evening; there it was—a macrodimensional creature lying in a spiral coil, breathing and speaking lines through the actors, just two indistinct parts of itself; motion and sound, masked in apparent significance, originated in the actors, the rest of its immense coiled form responding in ripples of laughter.

Lost in the transitions; terror, as familiar reality, sense of identity, safety, time, place and direction began to slip away.

Hot, humid, sticky atmosphere; our breath came in short, shallow gasps, oily smoke and harsh radiation burned through us.

Pain and fear soon gave way as we discovered that nothing worse was likely to happen ... as every experienced voyager knows, in the labyrinth, things are already as dangerous as they can get ... and they've always been that way.

We were acutely cognizant at this moment of the third line of the Voyager's Quatrain: "Not making any sudden moves"; it was like being in the presence of a big cat—a tiger, lion or an ocelot.

As prudent voyagers, we took especial care not to inflict primate mechanicality and human psycho-reflex into the situation; we already had the instinct for total attention-intensity even though we still lacked knowledge and direct experience; an oversight, a small mistake ... who knows what would have happened? ....

But it didn't happen; the experience was beautiful, elegant, nobody flubbed. Next time it might be different, but this time we listened and watched with fear and delight to that chilling rustling, that terrifying rippling undulation, that overwhelming feeling of majestic presence, as the dialogue and responding laughter rattled and rang through the quivering body of the enormous creature ... and lived to tell the tale.

Here end the notes collected from the experiment which successfully invoked the Simurgh.

The feathered serpent Quetzlcoatl, Malik the peacock, the wild boar, the Haida raven, the porcupine of the Iroquois, the great Norse bear, the Archangel Michael; an image formed by habit and experience, culture and circumstance....

What we see is fragmentary and incoherent, although when viewed from the point of view of the Absolute, to whom the totality of chaos is perfect order, it makes easy reading.

In the primate world, we attend a play, inattentively, unguardedly, blindly, stupidly. We ignore the tingle between the shoulder blades, the sure signals that something is breathing, watching, listening to itself.

The key to all this is in the breath. Breathing, posture, perfect mimicry, all these in elegant balance will bring us to the chamber of any macrobeing we may be courting at the moment.

Should we forget our breathing and lose the rhythm and the pulse, everything collapses; we, and not only we, suffer in anguish.

In the end, only thirty birds can find the Simurgh, The Great Peacock, because it is composed of thirty birds; not just any thirty birds ... each typicality must be represented.

In Armenian, the word *Groonk* means both "crane"— also a Buddhist symbol for the Absolute—and "the feeling of religiousness," not just personal but also in the sense of the sacred assembly.

We might be awestruck in the overwhelmingly majestic presence of the Absolute; profound feelings of religiousness are not uncommon; the atmosphere takes on a distinct quality, a glowing, self-luminescence similar to the light which descends to us from very high clerestory windows. The light has a crisp quality; it seems non-directional, yet brings objects into high relief.

Churches and cathedrals depend upon shafts of light, clouds of smoke, clarity and height, the illusion of magnitude, elevation and scale to evoke the feeling of religiousness in their congregations.

At what point do thirty birds become thirty—the Simurgh, just a bird inflated with unbreathable atmosphere? What becomes of the human primates during transubstantiation? Do they reach that chamber, or do they become lost in the rapture? . . . .

Now that we have been there once, what would allow us to make the journey again? In one chamber, thirty voyagers, in another, unimaginably distant, the Simurgh. Duplicability is a figment of the primate mind. We may make the experiment five hundred times, and only obtain the same result once. In so doing, we might begin to understand the terrible burden of being the Absolute.

There's no longer any doubt about the existence of other worlds. The real question is, how far is it from Midtown?

Woody Allen

E.J. GOLD, *ROOM WITH NO DOOR,*
PEN & INK WASH, 12''x9'', 1975.

CHAPTER 13

The Initiation of the Absolute

The Absolute is fragmented into an infinite number of parts which take the shape of a multi-dimensional labyrinth. The Absolute in the form of the Creation is the labyrinth through which we are voyaging. The Great Work is an attempt to bring the corpse of Creation to the most profound state of livingness.

In its native state, the Absolute exists only in relation to itself as the undifferentiated void, an ocean in a drop of water within water within water.

The Absolute has presence and attention, but not existence, a state quite apart from anything knowable to the human primate consciousness, although the subjective experience is available to the voyager in the consciousness of expanded morphology.

Undifferentiated as it is, the Absolute is able, even so, by a compounding process of self-induced semi-intentional shocks to form within itself at its epicenter, in its deepest attention-centrum, a high-energy plasma concentration contained and suspended in a basket-like magnetic web, a force-field of positron-active electroconductance, which in its containment forms an electrically viscous high-density particle field which we who dwell within it call *the universe,* or in our special language, *the Creation,* a class of universes containing all possible classes of universes in ascending and descending octavic order, manifesting on a common fundamental according to the laws governing the periodicity of harmonics and subtonics in the electromagnetic spectrum.

The Creation is spawned suddenly, automatically, always unexpectedly and spasmodically-involuntarily, existing not out of design but as a result of a reflexive reaction, a harsh, ironic, barking laugh in an empty sky . . . .

It is this ironic laughter, this spasmodic reflex at the alone-ness of it all which produces Creation; in a sense, Creation could be considered a gag-reflex reaction to absolutely nothing.

A simple, harmless exercise involving the use of a rubber mallet on an obliging friend's knee should serve adequately to illustrate the exact nature of involuntary reflex reactions, keeping in mind that this type of reaction is not limited to the muscle system of the biological machine.

Many involuntary spasmodic reflex reactions in the provinces of the body, emotions and the mind are known, and some people have dedicated their entire lives to the study and cataloging of these reflex reactions; an interesting hobby, but a sad commentary on contemporary science.

A secondary result is a type of macrocellular mitosis, fissioning of the Absolute—a self-produced "division between the waters and the waters," meaning simply that a buffer, the Creation, has been whomped up out of nothing, a sort of macrocellular creampuff, which maintains a workable separation between the Absolute and itself.

It is this high-energy plasma buffer which makes possible the relationship of the Absolute with itself in a cosmic lover-beloved balance game in which the Creation fulfills the function of an opposing gender sandwiched between the Absolute in its positive form and the Absolute in its negative-adversary form, thus avoiding the most profound taboo, self-annihilation by absorption into oneself, a taboo which, when translated into human primate terms expresses itself as narcissism and homophobia.

In this way, the Creation remains eternal because, once created, it exists without end, flowering repeatedly in periodic recurrence, always the same; same set, same play, same cast of characters.

Originating long before the Sumerian and Babylonian priests, an ancient tradition passes through the Egyptian, Zoroastrian, Mithraist and Indus Valley cultures.

In this ancient teaching, groups of shamanic voyagers formed themselves into living networks, clustered matrices of connective attention and mutually resolved and blended sensation, a geodesic syllogismobile, an expanded morphology to ascend cleanly into the macrodimensional, there to assume the morphology of the Absolute, catching other, lesser shamanic duties and obligation-tasks on the descent.

In the course of this ancient tradition a question was discovered, a question asked even today in some of the more obscure rabbinical teachings:

So, nu, during the Creation, what becomes of the Absolute ? The answer to this question forms the basis of the Great Work. During the Creation, the Absolute is entrapped by it because, although the Creation just happens by itself in reflex reaction, it is created *of* the Absolute; this idea is clearly expressed by the secret esoteric meditative phrase, *"I had nothing but myself with which to create the world; out of myself the world was made."* One consequence of which is that the Absolute temporarily loses the quality of *absoluteness* without losing the quality of *being* the Absolute.

The Absolute is caught up in the complex wave-formed plasma-suspension webwork of that mighty supercooled electromagnetic hydrogen we call the Creation which forces it into a descent from the Absolute-Absolute, its uncorrupted condition which it enjoyed immediately prior to Creation, although it couldn't have enjoyed it all that much or we wouldn't all be forced—along with the Absolute—to endure the somewhat messy result.

From the advent of Creation, the Absolute is slowly absorbed into the Creation, nailed inexorably to the plasma crucifix, each bound to the other, inseparable even with a crowbar, if we could find one sufficiently macro.

From this first rather inauspicious beginning, the Absolute is further enthralled by rapidly dancing illusions, its attention swept up in a continuous stream of distractions, and therefore becomes powerless to alter events within the Creation, even in a small, insignificant way.

All dimensions existing within the Creation are subtonic fragmentations of the Absolute, isolated and compartmentalized—only to the perceptions, not in topological reality—sections of the enormously complex body we call the Great Labyrinth which, viewed as a whole from outside itself takes the form of a clear drop of water; yet, from within, it seems an endless expanse of darkness filled with a vast, unimaginable quantity of matter and energy in an inexhaustible variety of forms.

Wherever we think we are able to go, we are destined to remain always inside the labyrinth, fumbling around in some dimension or other, however macro it might seem.

Along the same line of thought, if we ever happen to stumble into a position where we find ourselves actually able to work, we will slowly but inexorably become aware of much more than the rat's ultimate hope of escape; once we have learned to our satisfaction that escape is not the object, we can perhaps be useful to the Absolute and because of this, our eternal survival will become a necessity so that we may be able to perform our function. We may from the primate point of view feel that this is desirable, but after a while anything—even immortality—palls on one.

At some point in the development of our macrodimensional life, the option presents itself to sacrifice our normal destiny, which would have been a painless, joyful death, generally coming directly on the heels of a painful, joyless dying, as we permanently sever our ties to the Creation and reunite with the formless void in a return journey to the Absolute; total dissolution into the cosmic ocean of light.

We remain in this self-created hell, this aching separation only as long as we choose to remain in voluntary separation for the sake of the Work.

In this sense it would be accurate to view ourselves as computer RAM chips, random access modules which are, for the moment, changeable and vulnerable to reprogramming and erasure, striving to be permanently burned EPROM chips, read-only modules, unchangeable and inaccessible permanent crystallizations of programming and metaprogramming which will, if we are successful at our self-programming shamanic work, be secured with a Write-Protect shield, ensuring our unalterability, our utter inerasability, especially after the death of the primate self.

Our fate will thus be quite the opposite of those seeking escape, because we have—perhaps foolishly from the Wall Street Primate point of view—agreed to become a permanent fixture in the matrix of space.

On a totally different level, the human biological machine, within the context of an eternal Creation, partakes of the same eternalization; immortal in the worst possible way, destined to eternal existence in its own time, its own space; a frozen, four-dimensional configuration producing an illusion of activity and longevity; a time-tunnel to be voyaged; no change from outside, no change from inside, and no change will come of itself.

In the strictest sense, what we call the life of the machine is only another form of death; the biological machine is just as dead as the whole of Creation.

While the life of the machine partakes of death, the life of the essential self, a fragmented remnant of the Absolute engulfed in Creation, is the only part of Creation which can be said to be really alive.

We are destined to eternal rebirth in the Creation, forever chained to our corresponding primate selves, and we cannot get free of this automatically recycling rebirth except through the transformation of the essential self, and by transcending the life of the human primate, learning the life of the essential self, the eternal voyager, reaching the Heart of the Labyrinth and beyond....

When we think of eternity, we ordinarily understand it to mean *a very long time,* but eternity has nothing to do with time. We can think of eternity as a single, unfragmented tonic, the Creation existing forever at the primary tonic.

Time exists below the level of eternity; time can be viewed as a function of space, a perception by sensation of the next-higher macrodimension which, when perceived from the higher dimensional level includes in its formal configuration the totality of all possible events, a framework of frozen tableaus activated only by the passage of the voyaging essential self rummaging through the crystalline webwork of Creation, finding order and significance where there is none.

What we call time, experience and history are results of this voyaging, and the Creation will never lose these aspects so long as there are voyagers to pass through its endless hallways.

Perhaps an example set to music would help here . . . .

A whole note can be naturally or artificially divided into smaller fragments which produce a secondary inner octave within which we will inevitably find a harmonic fundamental corresponding relative to the secondary octave as did the original whole note to the first.

Each of those subtonics can be divided into further fragments which provide a tertiary set of octavic notes and still smaller fragments, each riddled with their own periodic harmonic fundamental frequency waveforms.

What we call "music" is a further fragmentation of harmonics along certain decreasing periodic scales— primary, secondary, tertiary, natural notes and harmonics, sub-harmonics, and overtones, producing an apparency of notes, subtractive frequencies, which are actually those sounds which happen to remain after the real sounds have mutually cancelled one another through various forms of beat-frequency oscillation.

We should be able to understand this better if we recall that what we call "color" is actually the reflection of rejected whole-spectrum white light, most of which has been absorbed by the pigmentation of the object. Pigment is what light is absorbed by the object. Color is whatever happens to remain after the light has been rejected by the object. Composite light, when it encounters any object, is broken up into its component parts and, according to the diffraction index of the object's surface, some components of composite light are absorbed, while others are reflected.

The color we see, therefore, is the only color that the object isn't. Objects themselves, their very form and substance, are the remains of wave-form cancellation. The original fundamental forms no longer exist by the time we are able to view them in the visible-light portion of the spectrum.

Even movement, which suggests the passage of time, is a fractional result of a tonic macrodimensional spatial configuration. In this sense, then, we can say that we never actually observe movement, we merely tend to connect a series of events and images, as a film, a series of still photographs, can suggest movement when projected at roughly one-thirtieth of a second, the visual image alternated with black.

In the same way, the careful observer will notice that the Creation flickers on and off in a measurable sixty-cycle hum, which produces that annoying lower-harmonic buzzing sound in the audible frequencies, commonly reported as *aum* or *om* and reminding one somewhat of an out-of-adjustment horizontal hold on a video monitor.

It is this sixty-cycle hum which produces what we voyagers disparagingly refer to as "the human-primate audible spectrum sounds" from which, through repetitive primate conditioning, human primates have learned to derive some significance and which gives the general impression— to a not particulary demanding audience—of some sort of rudimentary form of mutual communication.

The fragmentation of sound produces all matter, which can be thought of as slowed down light. In effect, we are walking mathematical equations, each a small part of an enormous but unexpressed—except in pure potential— mathematical equation which, in the end, regardless of exponential factors to which it was taken, still adds up to zero.

The macrocosmic machine which we call the Creation—not just the Creation at this moment in our subjective temporal perception but the Creation taken as a single object containing all time viewed as a form of spatial dimension—is the same in relation to the Absolute as our machine is to our essential self, and this is of utmost importance to the nonphenomenal voyager.

The essential self is similar to the Absolute, if not exactly the same as the Absolute, in terms of activities and general effects. The human biological machine and the being mirror the relationship between Creation and the Absolute. This is the only sense in which we can rightfully consider ourselves to be "made in the image of the Absolute".

Just as the human biological machine is to be found more or less perpetually in the sleeping state, likewise the Creation, considered as a machine, is also in a sleeping state, like dead meat on a hook.

We suffer in a sleeping machine, and we can imagine how the Absolute must also suffer in the face of an all-but-infinite and unbanishable lifeless, limp, unmoving, utterly unresponsive, unconscious and inattentive dead thing.

How utterly astounding to realize the predicament of the Absolute through our own experience of the invincible power of the momentum of the machine. Imagine the crushing power and momentum of Creation in the maintenance of its corpselike state.

How can the Absolute hope to encourage the Creation—*of its own will*—to life? This in technical terms is called—but only on the highest macrodimensional level, from the Absolute to the Creation—*The Invitation* .

The secret of The Invitation is well-kept, given only by initiation; it is soundless, undetectable by word or deed; it has no gesture, no visible prompting, yet the invitation is clear: to awaken, to come to life.

As the human biological machine can become a transformational apparatus by being brought to life, awakened, Creation can also become a transformational apparatus for the Absolute in the same way, and what real hope can there be for the Absolute other than utilization of the Creation as an evolutionary apparatus, considering that nothing within Creation will ever change? . . . .

The machine has a will of its own, and because the Creation is related by corresponding to the machine, we know that it must also have a will of its own, equally powerful and unbreakable and, like the human biological machine, also seeks the dark lethargic sleep of forgetfulness, the touch of *Lethe*, the bringer of death, the ultimate steady-state at the deepest depths of the entropic totem pole.

We know that the essential self has two—and only two—genuine powers: the will of attention and presence, and that these two acts of will are sufficient forces in the awakening of the human biological machine, responding as it does to the compelling pressure of attention by coming to life, and in the same way, as voyagers, shamanic workers, we can and must learn to develop will of attention and presence and apply these to the awakening of the Creation.

The Absolute is dependent upon the shamanic voyager, an individualized consciously functioning fraction of itself, for this service . . . .

It is not sufficient that the Absolute simply be aware of itself, its presence and attention existing independently of Creation; it could not be expected to deduce from this or from anything else in its experience that the Creation could be brought to life by the power of attention, nor that this would cause it to begin to function as a transformational apparatus. But we have had this experience. If we could bring the Creation to life often enough, eventually, perhaps, by example, the Absolute might make the intuitive connection . . . .

This brings us back to the age-old communication problem of the mystic, for whom it's difficult to communicate the visions of the real world to human primates, but this problem pales in comparison to the difficulty of communicating to the Absolute, beyond all—even the highest—dimensional levels.

How ironic, this reversal of the Prometheus problem; no one can stand before the Absolute without experiencing total annihilation; yet we must find a way to make the Absolute aware of Creation, but in the fullest possible detail, the totality of all potential attention.

Meanwhile, the Absolute is aware of Creation, painfully aware; it's a fact, it's there, but it's dead, horrible, unconfrontable, a rotting corpse, yet what else is there to love, to keep company in the emptiness of the void?

This should begin to throw light on the Great Work and why communication to the Absolute is both necessary and difficult. The Absolute can't derive answers—it doesn't know where to look. It has no reference library—*we are the reference library,* but it can't reach down to our dimension with its enormously scaled attention . . . .

We, as part of Creation, can perform the basic and practical research—and communicate the results of our research to the Absolute by the performance of the awakening process. Attention is beyond scale, and the attention of a shamanic voyager is equally effective in the macrodimensions.

The Absolute is suffering in an unknowable way . . . unknowable until we also experience it in the place of the Absolute, possible only for a daring and courageous voyaging shaman.

A human primate, who has always been just one faceless part of an enormous, swarming herd of similar cow-like creatures, can't know what real loneliness is, but we who are labyrinth voyagers can leave the herd, and *feel* its fullblown intensity—an unforgettable and deeply disturbing experience with questionable value to anyone but the most determined shaman.

It may be upsetting to think of the Absolute as a frightened child sitting in the dark, waiting for the bogeyman, like the Olmec boy-god, seated in frozen, terra-cotta fear and wonder.

From time to time it may relax, its anxiety and dread washed away for the moment as the Creation comes to life and in this moment of companionship, its fear and longing for some form of parental soothing may be relieved.

This may seem a clumsy anthropomorphic way of describing the Absolute, but really everything in the higher dimensions, and beyond dimension, in the Absolute, is— except for scale—very similar to the primate in form, configuration and appearance. It's not the form that's disturbing, but deeper things, things not visible or evident to the inattentive.

In order to understand the basis for human primate inattention, we could consider a story about a man who dies and goes to heaven and is told by the gatekeeper that he doesn't have quite enough points to get into heaven, but that if he is able to remain awake, the gate of heaven opens every hundred years, and if he can slip in on one of those occasions, then he can be accepted into heaven.

Accordingly, he leans against the wall and because nothing happens right away, he promptly drifts off, first into vague daydreams and then, inevitably, into a deep dreaming sleep. His dreams are rudely interrupted by the sound of the gate slamming shut . . . .

Why did he fall asleep since, being dead and all, he didn't really need sleep? The typical primate reaction to apparent absence of change—which is to say, change which is not demandingly obvious—is a form of unconsciousness called sleep, which can take many subtle and not-so-subtle forms.

If we lock ourselves in a room in which nothing happens except that we get fed three times a day, the most important event, upon which we will tend to focus almost the whole totality of our attention and expectation, will be mealtimes; when we're not eating, thinking about eating, preparing to eat or comparing our present meal with memories of other, past meals and fantasies about possible future meals, we'll fall helplessly and unknowingly into one form of sleep or another, deeply horizontal or daydreamingly vertical. In its own way, the Absolute faces a similar situation.

We can try to imagine what it would feel like to exist in the total absence of stimulation; no conversation, no books, no records, no tapes, no sounds, no images, no sensations except one—a sort of nagging, pulling, magnetic, slow but inexorable downward sucking effect, or we can voyage to the macrodimension in which this is really happening . . . to us.

How can the Absolute avoid the magnetic seduction of sleep, which we call the Creation, since it finds itself entrapped *every time*? The fact is, it's up to us to extricate the Absolute, and that can only be by evolution, which begins with encouraging the Creation to bring itself to life and this self-initiation—which means, not activated by the Absolute but by itself, as a self-initiating and inner-directed being—can only be brought about by the continual pressure of concentrated attention and presence, the adoration, The Invitation.

One would think that once burned, twice learned and all that, but how can the Absolute learn anything when it's all obliterated by the absolute Truth of Emptiness.

It's our task to somehow, in some unimaginable inexpressible language of communication, by suggestion, by example, entice the Absolute *to place its full and profound totality of attention on the Creation* with the fullest possible intensity—the only type of attention available to the Absolute, as it happens—and to wait patiently and without alarm as the Creation uses this attention to bring itself out of death and into the waking state and is thus activated as a transformational apparatus on the absolute level.

As we perform the action within the labyrinth, it occurs correspondingly in the highest, *as* the labyrinth—the center is the circumference, the macrocosm and microcosm, seed and tree, and all that sort of Sufi-Buddhist-Hindu poetic jargon.

We are capable of identifying with the machine; not only capable, but naturally inclined to do so, and what is the Creation if not a machine, just like our own machine, but on a much larger and more annoying scale.

Imagine a deaf, dumb and blind child who has never seen, never heard, never spoken, and is completely unaware of anything but itself and that only vaguely, for a variety of reasons. How do we get through, and not just get the attention of the child—anyone can do that—but convey subtle and complex ideas?

Now imagine being a tiny little ant trying to get the attention of a human, because you know something that the human didn't know that would be to the great benefit of the human, if only the human would pay attention to the little ant. You can't speak the human's language; you haven't got the equipment with which to communicate to the human on the human level; you have only the equipment of an ant.

First, you've got to get the human's attention, which brings us to a story:

One of the regulars of the Cafe Tepozton had spent many years in prison. In the first year he succeeded in remaining relatively sane but by the second year he began to go completely "stir-crazy", but he was saved by the appearance of a little ant making its way slowly across the cell floor.

He put a piece of paper in front of the ant and it climbed on. He found a box of matches and took out the matches and kept the ant inside. He made a little bed and some furniture for the ant and put them in the match box with the ant.

He made some circus equipment—hoops, barrels, balancing bars and even a miniature suspension wire—for the ant , and that gave him an idea. The ant that he had named Harry became more than just a pet. Harry the ant represented an opportunity for him to really make a comeback in life, to give his life new meaning. With the right promotion of the microscopic circus act, he could even become a millionaire.

He taught Harry every trick he could think of. Harry was so intelligent that he could answer elementary problems of mathematics. He could add and subtract. He could even multiply and divide, and do a few fractions.

By the time he was released from prison, his pet ant, Harry, could almost speak. Finally the day of his release arrived. He was given five dollars and a new suit of clothes.

He put on the suit and pocketed the five dollars, and very carefully carried the match box with Harry inside in one hand and in the other he carried a box full of the miniature circus equipment.

He could hardly wait to get to the Cafe Tepozton to show his friends his spectacular circus act. He knew they had never seen anything like it before. After all, who has the time to train an ant to such a degree? It takes years of intensive training—hour after hour, day after day.

When he entered he was very happy to see his old friends and grateful that Juan hadn't sold the cafe to someone else. He only had five dollars and he knew Juan wouldn't charge him too much since he had just gotten out of prison. He even thought of a way to get out of paying altogether... Harry could perform on the bar!

He opened the matchbox with the circus equipment. He took out a tweezers from his pocket, and carefully laid out the circus equipment in a circle about ten centimeters in diameter. Then he opened the match box containing Harry, and very carefully he lifted Harry out of the match box and placed him on the bar near the circus equipment.

"Hey, everybody, come see this," he announced. Everybody gathered around.

He said, "Juan, do you see this ant?"

"No problem," said Juan, grinding his thumb on the bar, making jelly out of the ant beneath his thumb. "I got the filthy little thing!"

We employ imagery and fantasy to explain to ourselves what we are unable to see until we can actually see it. The totality of all possible attention is far simpler than the vivid but incomplete picture painted by the mind.

The ancient shamen from Sumer and Babylon understood this, and had obtained firsthand knowledge that the Creation is an involuntary effect, that the existence of the Creation was not for the benefit of human primates. They understood also that the Absolute is the all-pervading living spirit which is caught up in its own involuntary Creation.

This idea is found also in Manichaeism, Gnosticism, Hinduism, Buddhism, Lamaism, Egypto-Roman deification, Pharaonic deification, esoteric Christianity, Jewish mystical teachings and several contemporary lower Manhattan spiritual doctrines.

The shamen learned how to produce a long term change on the Creation itself, which without this change would remain fixed, crystallized. This thing they learned, we now call *binding in the Kingdom* .

What change is possible within a fixed and crystallized Creation? No change is possible where time and space are not, which is to say, in a pure mathematical causality.

Yet binding in the Kingdom is a shamanic fact; what is *bound* in the lower dimensions has an effect in the macrodimensions.

The concept of the Great Work originated as far back as Babylon and Sumer; the idea of helping the Absolute to accomplish something, the definition of which it is the province of this volume to provide.

What can a voyager, who arises from the human primate, do to help a being who is *not* in time and space and *has* no time and space; has life—such as it is—in one single breath, and whose every breath produces a new—but not different—cycle of Creation?

A definite change of being is possible for us, and if we are capable of evolution then it must also be possible for the Absolute; imagine what this hope must mean to an unchanging eternal involuntary Creator confronted with a lifeless corpse upon which it must eternally fix its gaze; its pain must be all the more because for a while, a moment or two, the Creation has sometimes come to life.

THE SPEED OF LIGHT

Love is the speed of light.
The Absolute is love.
The Absolute is the speed of light.
The speed of light is stillness and silence.
The Absolute is stillness and silence.
Love is stillness and silence.
Where is stillness?
Between motion.
Where is silence?
Between sound.
Where is the Absolute?
Between motion and sound.
Silence between every sound.
Stillness between every motion.

E.J. GOLD, *NORTON STREET,* PEN & INK WASH, 9''x 12'', 1975.

CHAPTER 14

The Labyrinth Voyager's Quatrain

All phenomena is illusion.
Neither attracted nor repelled.
Not making any sudden moves.
My habits will carry me through.

The voyager's quatrain is the most powerful tool for voyaging in the labyrinth. A detailed examination of each line in the quatrain can help us better understand several aspects of the voyage as well as the connection between the labyrinth and the Absolute which we have already mentioned.

All phenomena is illusion refers to phenomena as a totality—not as a series of individual phenomena, therefore the use of the singular verb is not a colloquialism, but semantic exactitude.

Neither attracted nor repelled. A good illustration of the full consequences of what this means can be found in a contemporary movie entitled *Raiders of the Lost Ark.* In this otherwise strictly entertaining movie, the Ark of the Covenant is opened, revealing the invoked presence of God.

One of the Nazis looks up and sees something heading toward him. To him, it looks at first blush like a pretty woman. Of course what he's really looking at is the Shekinah onto which he is projecting his own subjective imagery. This projection originates in the machine and is as short-lived as the attention span of the machine itself.

As it wears off, his vision is no longer cloaked in human form, and he reacts with fear at such an inhuman sight. This is not at all surprising; the direct presence of God is to the creatures of the Creation what a cuttinghead acetylene torch is to a paper bag. Once there is nothing separating him from this higher presence, he is then free to cave in from the psychic, emotional and organic effects of the full force of his reaction to fear.

His organic tensions cause the machine to become a frozen field, thus stopping and absorbing the radiation. He could have, with just a little training and discipline, allowed the vibrations to simply cause the machine's electrical field and liquid concentrations to go temporarily out of phase or stasis without reacting—as unpleasant as it might have been.

This vibration resembles the kind of effect that occurs at very high speeds in a race car. Many feelings of reaction to such effects will present themselves as one voyages through the labyrinth. We may not particularly like these effects, but we can learn to endure, and even to enjoy them, improbable as it may seem to us at present.

Any vehicle will be more or less unstable at high velocity where there is inertia, and the slightest overreaction can cause an immediate disaster.

This brings us to the third line: *Not making any sudden moves.* This should be self-evident.

During the course of a voyage it is important to know which actions are appropriate, and which ones actually bring the voyage to a grinding halt. Every time we produce a malaprop, we're forcing expulsion from the macrodimension and re-entry into the lower.

One can experience this phenomenon in everyday life: in cooking, in dealing with children, in the middle of a sale to a client, one can always tell when something has gone wrong; falling out of orbit can occur at any time. If it happens to us quite commonly in the ordinary course of events, it's just as likely to occur in our labyrinthine voyages. There is an expression to remember, *Wandering is not voyaging.*

The fourth line, *My habits will carry me through,* tells us that *if* all phenomena is illusion, *and* we're neither attracted nor repelled, *and* we make no sudden moves, *then* let our habits carry us through.

If all phenomena is illusion, that means we perceive it fully, not just vaguely. All phenomena is illusion means I perceive *all* phenomena *as a whole,* not just bits and pieces, not just local phenomena. It doesn't mean *almost* all phenomena. It doesn't say, all phenomena is illusion *except* for my son, my daughter, my automobile . . . .

Under what circumstances would one be likely to perceive all phenomena as a whole? This is something we don't need in the human sector. We are able to perceive all phenomena only in chambers which are in themselves composites of all phenomena.

There are not many chambers of this sort. In fact there is only one chamber which is almost infinitely reassembled. One chamber which when disassembled can be reconstructed in a slightly different format to obtain a new matrix, not created but synthesized out of the same stuff as the first chamber. The first chamber doesn't cease to exist; once it exists, it exists in eternity. Once it has been made, it imprints and what remains is an after-image. The after-image doesn't degenerate because there's no wear and tear, no entropy, no opposition, no friction, no resistance to it, and so it remains in this timeless eternal state.

What causes Creation in the first place is what we call God, in a particular form which we may visualize as a name, an attribute, or, giving form, dimension and substance, a chamber. In this respect, matter doesn't truly exist except as an after-image, a residual phenomenon of light after the passage of the livingness of God through the firmament of the void. However, it's not affected by deterioration or decay. Decay, in fact, is non-existent because matter is already decayed—slowed down—light. Then further decay takes another form in the continuing fractionings of the Absolute.

The first decay in the intensity of the tonic occurs in the form of an after-image. The second decay is in the form of a fractioning, forming much lower harmonics and overtones which, in the larger wavelengths, result in soundwaves when transmitted through a plastic medium, whether solid, liquid, or gaseous, and which in even longer wave structures result in systems transmittable through vacuum in the absence of any but electromagnetic media, and which in somewhat median frequencies can result in above-visible light spectrum sub-etheric high-energy plasma time-reversal phenomena, forming special local-field physics in the hydrogen-to-sodium range.

The third decay is the apparent deterioration of form due to a subtonic retardation. And the fourth decay is a loss of energy in itself . . . dimming toward darkness.

Creation is not one thing that happened after another, but rather an inevitable event that occurred as the Absolute tumbled through a series of form changes, all imposed one upon the other in and as the same matrix, all co-existing simultaneously, one on top of the other like an impossibly complex folded tesseract.

But while we who are within the Creation seem to hold one form, we're only attuned to three spatial dimensions and one temporal dimension; from our limited view, nothing else exists beyond this.

We tend to view our passage from one form of spatial structure to another as a corridor, but there is no corridor; it's just an alteration of form. Since they all occupy the same space but not the same dimensions, all chambers interface equally with all other chambers, providing total instantaneous accessibility to all possible forms from any other form.

All planes, angles and points mutually coincide within the Creation which can be conceptualized as a series of cubes folded in on themselves to make a single cube, where the surfaces of each cube coexist with all other cubes, something like a Klein bottle composed of a single surface and, technically speaking, no volume whatever.

A moebius strip is a section of a Klein bottle; a Klein bottle can be sectioned into an infinite number of moebius strips. We can think of the entire Creation as a Klein bottle.

The universe—by which we mean the observable phenomenal aspect of Creation which can be observed with the standard biological visual apparatus or captured through telescopes—is only one four-dimensional cross-section of a nearly infinitely multidimensional totality of non-temporal instantaneously eternal Creation. If ever we are able to construct extremely high performance telescopes, we'll see only one single section of the Creation because the universe, as experienced in the primate levels of perception, lacks other dimensions beyond the three spatial dimensions we can see and measure and the single linear temporal dimension which we can only sense.

As we are now, we are utterly incapable of moving out of the simple four-dimensional universe and into the higher magnitudes of Creation; certainly, we're not ordinarily equipped to upscale beyond the Creation itself.

But it's all so easy if we know how—even an enormous quantum leap into unimaginable multidimensional fields is not that great a step. When one perceives correctly, one sees all phenomena as a whole, because all of Creation is apparent. One sees the illusion of line-of-horizon dimensionality.

Ironically, the fact that one can see all phenomena as illusion is itself an illusion; the obvious, observable immediate perception that all phenomena is visible—is an illusion; that one is seeing all phenomena is illusion, and the phenomena that one is seeing is an illusion... Mystics have traditionally had a lot of trouble explaining this one, and it's not going all that well for me, either....

Neither attracted nor repelled; attracted to what? Repelled by what? Obviously, phenomena; what we can see, smell, touch, taste, sense. Its attractive and repellant nature indicates that we're identifying with it, and are for the time being unable to see it clearly as an illusion. We have identified with a phenomenon within the phenomenal structure and, in doing so, we demonstrate that we have missed the meaning and importance of the first idea, that *All phenomena is illusion*.

If one perceives all phenomena as illusion, then one is able to be neither attracted nor repelled because *phenomena is phenomena*.

Let's examine the third line, *Not making any sudden moves*. What constitutes a sudden move? A sudden move goes counter to whatever happens to be happening at the moment. It will break the flow of the chamber, of the action, of the continuity. If we're in motion and we stop, that's a sudden move, and so is any change that is not appropriate, anything which does not belong—an out-of-place thing, an anomaly, a malaprop, a sudden alteration in characteristic or in the general ambience.

Not making any sudden moves encompasses a variety of reactions like shrieking, coming to a sudden halt when in motion, pulling back, jumping, turning, twisting, robotic, hypnagogic prattle, throwing up on the invocant. None of these moves are in themselves to be considered sudden—it is always a question of context which will decide whether or not what we did or stopped doing falls into the category of "sudden moves".

One can always hear the clunk of a wrong move, feel the impact of re-entry, and see the signs at the recovery area . . . *Welcome back to Earth, please extinguish all dazzling and self-luminous lights* . . . As the machine reintegrates itself into the customary four dimensions, we will come to see how thick the darkness is over our eyes . . . .

Consider the fourth line once again, *My habits will carry me through*. Whose habits? . . . And what is it through which they'll carry me? We already know about the rebound effect—the machine habits will reflex us back to the human sector. We can depend on them to saturate us with the somnambulant state. *Our machine's habits and its implac-*

able will and insatiable hungers are our return ticket. This is very convenient because we don't really want to stay in foreign territory all that long. We want to stay where we live like cockroaches.

The question inevitably presents itself, *Why are we voyaging?* We can get seriously—though perhaps not permanently—damaged electronically and electrically. We can blow circuits; synaptic connections can fuse, creating a permanent imbalance in the machine and reducing or destroying its value as a transformational apparatus.

If we use the machine little by little as a transformational apparatus, it will accustom itself to the fusion process, until no protective membrane remains between the immediate on-line brain awareness of the machine and the full memory and attention of the essential self.

If the habits of the essential self are the same as the machine's, then we're not going anywhere, but if they're different from the machine's—but only to the extent that they're different—the voyage will extend beyond the four dimensions of the human sector.

In this sense, the statement *My habits will carry me through* means that the voyager's habits—the voyager defined as the essential self—will insure that I will get to where I need to go.

Eventually, our machine-habits will drop away, and when they do, our habits as a voyager will be the only habits that remain. However, *this is only true if we're slated for the Work. If the habits of the essential self can be brought into alignment with the Work, then we are swept up and carried to exactly where we need to be.*

A shaman in the Work is like a cockroach without a home. No longer can we hide out with the other sleepwalking, eternally hungry and perturbed cockroaches in one big, milling mass of flesh. This means that we will be permanently on the road, radically underpaid but constantly roving interdimensional trouble-shooters.

How does one encourage new habits in the essential self, since one can't get at the essential self directly? We need to use the machine as a transformational apparatus, which naturally programs the essential self to perform work-functions in the multi-dimensional labyrinth. Let's go back to the question about the differences between the universe and the Creation.

Each chamber is a cube, an all-but-mathematical-and-topological part of a folded tesseract, a nearly infinite number of cubes folded in upon themselves, in which each plane and angle is coincident with every other, all adjacent, all equally interfaced.

Sometimes the only connection is through interstices, a junction of planes rather than an interplanar crossing.

Think of the Creation as a very complex equation composed in turn of very simple sub-structures—an algebraic geometric matrix built upon a totally known falsehood. The basic axiom, when effectively buried, produces the effect of existence and, when fully recalled either intentionally or accidentally, causes its complete disintegration, at which point it becomes a high-energy non-material potential.

Creation is the remaining after-image of something which we can never know or experience directly and survive to tell the tale. We can never actually see the "first cause", the passage of which or whom made this Creation come into existence in descending octavic orders of diminishing subtonic chords. We do happen to catch a glimpse of it now and then and, sure enough, its effects are always devastating. We call the effect that it has on us "death".

This brings us back to the idea of Creation as an equation. Suffice it to say for the moment that Creation is a giant equation, held in place by nothing in particular, and fixated by itself.

It should be understood that this multiplex equation is not an expression of the Creation, it *is* the very nature of Creation, which is, speaking in absolute or near-absolute terms, a pure abstract mathematical construct.

Fragmentations and decay elements and their resultant fractionings occur at predictable intervals within the

Creation, but the Creation itself, in its first appearance as an after-image, can entropically decay no further. As a whole, in its totality, it does not fraction.

Fractionings which do occur are internal and have no effect on the primary. The secondary, tertiary, and quaternary fractionings or decays have no effect on the whole until the very last entropic decrease. The after-image, relative to its internal fractionings, remains the same until the very bottom of the energy-well, until the energy dissipates entirely, at which point everything goes black, and a strange reverberating voice utters in the darkness, "Hey, who turned out the lights?" or something to that effect. Creation runs out of heat—no longer is it able to exchange heat.

As for ourselves, using basic shamanistic principles, we can move forward, back, side to side, up and down, in this multi-dimensional labyrinth, and we're not limited to approximately infinite directional capability... We can remove ourselves from the system entirely, if we have access to an out-of-system corresponding function, a functional existence apart from the dimensional levels from which we emerged. The system manages itself; but our familiarity is entirely limited to system management.

Fortunately, the system is also designed to manage something outside itself, otherwise it would be useless for our purposes.

The odd thing is, the thing outside itself and the thing inside itself are one and the same, a closed circuit, a single dimension which fractions downward into itself, into other dimensions. If this set of descending scales—circles within circles—is too difficult to comprehend, we can always take comfort in the thought that actually, when we get right down to it, there's really nothing here at all.

In the dimensionless dimension of the Absolute, "Hello! Is anyone out there?", is an echo.

One must descend at least three levels to get a change in the return echo. Of course, we mustn't forget—although we might prefer to—that anything other than a direct echo is an alteration of perception, not an alteration of what is actually there; the fact remains there really is nobody there, except the multitude within the Absolute.

The question really comes down to: *what business do we have out there in the labyrinth,* if any, Mr. and Mrs. Cockroach? Why are we crawling around in other dimensional levels? What is our purpose?

In our search for the Heart of the Labyrinth, once we've found it, all we will have accomplished is that *we will have seen and experienced what caused the labyrinth.*

Even if we manage to reach the Heart of the Labyrinth—and this is quite an accomplishment—we will undoubtedly scuttle in fear or confusion or both, back to the human sector many, many times before we are able to remain easily in the heart, and pass out of it on our voyages into macrodimensions in which we have found useful work and, therefore, continued existence in service.

At first our natural tendencies to downscale will lead us back to safe territory, and yet perhaps sooner than we expect—we will no longer return to the human sector. The Heart of the Labyrinth, known as the Middle Pillar, or Grand Central Station, will become our base of operations, our only home. We will find the Heart of the Labyrinth and make our nest there, and from then on, make excursions from the heart outward and back again.

The Heart of the Labyrinth is not a maudlin, drunken, romanticized, sentimental, sobbing, goopy mood.

It is a swooning mood; the mood that mystics tried to explain without ever quite being able to, but I'm going to. It's "as if" sentimental, maudlin, romantic, but it isn't. It's coldly logical with a sense of beauty, a sense of irony, and a sense of humor all taken together, a sweeping, falling effect without descending into unconsciousness.

It's hard to understand this emotion if one has never experienced it. It's the emotion which is the whole point of monastic life, the emotion of The Man on the Cross. If we can climb into this emotion, we will find ourselves at the Heart of the Labyrinth. The cross is associated with the heart because the Sacred Heart describes so clearly the mood of the Heart of the Labyrinth.

The yogi achieves the Heart of the Labyrinth by seeking the vision through silence, inaction, recognition, non-wanting, the non-desire for the Heart of the Labyrinth. When we're at the Heart of the Labyrinth, there is nothing to desire or to achieve.

From the Heart of the Labyrinth, where there is no achievement and no desire, is it possible to work? Can we leave the Heart of the Labyrinth with no purpose, no goal, no desire, no reward in sight...*Can we work anyway?* That's an important idea.

A Boddhisatva is *able* to leave the place of enlightenment to work in spite of a complete lack of desire and necessity to strive toward the future...because the Work *does* exist and *is* necessary.

We'll laugh when we see the irony of our achievement—the Heart of the Labyrinth! Let's hope it's not an insane giggle! That's one danger associated with sarcastic voyagers—they inevitably go insane in the Heart of the Labyrinth, because they have so much fear, but no sense of humor to accept the futility of primate-driven purposes; they aren't able to accept *purpose for its own sake.*

At the very Heart of the Labyrinth, where one could expect things to have so much importance, the Work toward which we are striving will seem to have a double aspect: on the one hand it will be perceived as an absolute necessity—and on the other hand, it will seem to be *without* necessity. We must be prepared to face this paradox without being crushed by it.

Any competent voyager makes use of the mood of a chamber to locate a chamber or a dimension, following the mood to the chamber in which that mood is the atmosphere; the atmosphere, after all, *is* the mood.

The atmosphere of a chamber will also have a unique odor. Odor is part of mood. Odor is an electrical phenomenon related to ozone, and exerts its effect because both the machine and the atmosphere are electrical fields. When we change the atmosphere, we also make subtle alterations in the electrical field. We can create an atmospheric sawtooth wave with smell such as is created by a sharp odor. We also can be aware of gentle odors and mellow tones. Everything we know of as a phenomenon is detectable in terms of waves, therefore in terms of odor.

Essential oils can be used to create an atmospheric odor which can help us to track a particular chamber, dimension or direction; we can find a particular chamber by following its smell.

Through mood, it is similarly possible to locate, with some precision, any chamber in the labyrinth. One needn't have to have been there before to infer its existence.

Another way that one can find a chamber is by seeking a high-pitched sound, something like a distant smoke-alarm, and following the sound to the chamber where it originates. There is an extensive array of means at our disposal to locate any chamber, and a nearly infinite number of chambers . . . .

Many chambers have similar smells and many more fractionings on either side of those also have similar smells. Aromatics with limited tones that produce fewer accidental harmonics will produce greater locational exactitude.

The more tones, the more harmonics generated; the fewer the tones generated, the fewer harmonics, and the less farther afield we will tend to drift in our voyaging. Each subtone we eliminate directs us more precisely toward a fundamental tone. Statistically speaking, when we've narrowed it down from an almost infinite number of chambers to a mere four-hundred trillion, we have almost identified the chamber.

If, in addition, one is intensely familiar with the mood associated with the chamber, then it will be just that much easier to locate and land there. We are all too familiar with the overwhelming drenching mood of the Heart of the Labyrinth, and if we are not overwhelmed by the sweetness of death, we can easily detect and find our way to it.

The mood itself is relatively pleasant, but not the intensity. Most voyagers try to get accustomed to the teeth-gritting intensity, but it never does get any easier. A really fine wine has to be kept within a tolerance of a few degrees either way, but cockroaches, unlike your above-average Cabernet Sauvignon '73, can tolerate vast extremes of fluctuating temperatures, humidity, and radiation. They're a very hardy species; they will undoubtedly survive the next nuclear war—there's already been one in 1945, in case you hadn't noticed—and evolve into an intelligent species, so they'll be the first . . . If by then we haven't learned the Work in human primate form, perhaps we can learn it as a cockroach! . . . .

Quality or type of sound can also help us to detect a chamber—a gong-like ringing, a siren-like sound, a clucking, clicking, clacking; the distant hum of a star drive . . . a strange languorous buzzing . . . the imperative nagging blare of an Excedrin commercial; a fanfare and roaring crowd sounds as someone wins the fifteen-million-dollar pyramid . . . .

Qualities of light and dark can also be employed in the detection of chambers; such qualities as hue, tone, pastels, gray scale, all have meaning in the description of certain exact atmospheres, as do humidity, chill, clammy heat, balmy breeze, oppressive heat . . . Light quality can be influenced by almost anything; something as incongruous as a television set, a candle; a sparkling ray of sunshine peeking through a crack in the curtain . . . .

A combination of such elements can get us to our destination if it provides us with all the notable qualifiers of a particular space. Each detail added to the overall picture narrows down the options: this sound, this light-quality, this atmospheric quality, this odor, this temperature . . . .

These are all easily perceivable phenomena, but in addition we must become aware of the unperceivable, though measurable, phenomena. Mood is an essential ingredient in the atmosphere of any chamber, yet how does one even begin to describe the qualities of mood that we evoke within ourselves and with which we influence the uterine ambience of our immediate surroundings? We have at best a superficial acquaintance with mood; and we habitually limit our total possible repertoire of emotions.

What is a mood? We know it has to do with combinations of emotions and state of mind. So far, this is still part of the human sector experience...But how does one convey the compelling quality of higher and much more subtle moods such as are encountered in non-human spaces? How does one express and notate for another these unique moods that transcend anything in our ordinary experience?

The more exalted moods are not ordinarily accessed. As far as human primates are concerned, macrodimensional thoughts, emotions and moods are so foreign that they tend to be relegated as a rather disreputable member of the general categorical class of mysticism—a convenient way to label something unknown and to avoid dealing with our own limitations of emotional repertoire in which we are all but cripples. Words are useless in any attempt at clarity and accuracy in a description of even the most ordinary of macrodimensional moods....

What enables the flow from mood to mood? How to describe the rich subtleties of intensity, the fine texture of exaltation? Each mood is different from the other; all have their distinguishing qualities...As we remain huddled like hairless rats in the four-dimensional human sector, our moods resemble those of the smaller, Norwegian variety of rat—fearful, suspicious, protective, grasping, restless, easily irritated, and savage, and destructive as an automatic result. If we venture outward, we discover an incredibly rich palette of emotional coloration.

The mood of greatest immediate interest is that unique mood which imposes itself at the Heart of the Labyrinth. As for the deep, almost intolerably excruciating intensity of the emotional transmissions at the Heart of the Labyrinth, very little guidance can be provided to help us find our balance beforehand.

For obvious reasons, we want to decrease the potential for regret at ending up in the wrong chamber. Even so, we will find many lookalike chambers but there's really nothing else like the chamber at the very heart.

To get anywhere at all in the labyrinth beyond where one is, one must pass through the heart, no matter where the starting point.

Inevitably we must pass through the Heart of the Labyrinth even if we're just moving through to an adjacent chamber; we must go to the Heart of the Labyrinth and then out, in the course of voyaging.

A certain part of our course will follow ley lines between chambers, but then, eventually, we'll be brought to the Heart of the Labyrinth, and then work outward again.

The Heart of the Labyrinth occupies the very center of the labyrinth, and yet it is the labyrinth in its totality—both the epicenter and the circumference. This is important to remember because *when we're in the center, we're not just in the Heart of the Labyrinth, we are the labyrinth itself as a whole.* This orientation enables us to get around in the labyrinth with a little lapel badge that says *You are here.* We orient ourselves in the Heart of the Labyrinth and head in approximately the wrong direction; this "drunkard's walk" will take us to our temporary destination much more rapidly than a straight-line traversement.

Mathematically speaking, the drunkard's walk is more or less the same as Brownian motion—a series of random motions of microscopic particles suspended in a liquid or gas. Each particle travels randomly in one direction for some distance, and then in another random direction for another random distance, randomity being rather strictly defined as a point of energy-transfer as found in particle collision.

One can eliminate random motion in the labyrinth insofar as one is *able* to obey the second line, *Neither attracted nor repelled.* Attractions and repulsions will create "as if" Brownian motion, in which case, we will be forced—aesthetically speaking—to banish whatever vestigial dark forces are around or within us at the moment, exorcising ourselves of those nefarious demons of Maxwell's, just in order to be able to move freely from one point in the labyrinth to another. It is Maxwell's demons which produce the drunkard's walk.

In connection with this, evocation and invocation are defined in a slightly different way; invocation is the act of drawing down from a macrodimension, while evocation is the act of drawing upward from whatever dimension we're sitting in at the moment.

In that sense, demonic figures are simply beings of lower dimensions, as they appear to us in the dimension into which they've been drawn.

Of course, in their own native dimension, they appear neither demonic nor horrible except to the practiced eye of the prejudiced beholder. Angelic or celestial figures, on the other hand, happen to appear glowing and radiant only because they were drawn down from a macrodimension.

In the macrodimensions, we also appear somewhat demonic, depending on how we got there. If we were drawn there, we'll have taken on demonic characteristics from having been forced upward through the dimensions. When drawn up, we grow horny protuberances and our outer electrical layer, the skin, becomes thick, rough and scaly, while the voice becomes unaccountably smooth and compelling. Drawn downward, the form tends to glow and radiate, and the voice becomes rough and gravelly; the general appearance is rather radiant, as opposed to dark.

To further eliminate random motion in our labyrinthine explorations we can learn to rely on our essential self attention. Machine attention is measurable in units. The brain has insufficient attention units to spread over entire chambers; it is limited to only as much detail as it can perceive in an individual object. The only way to perceive the necessary clarity of detail is through a being-brain bypass.

We must force ourselves to observe far beyond the limits of the machine, to bypass the machine perceptions. This is especially necessary for labyrinth voyaging because only with that amount of detail can we correctly navigate. In some cases, we will constrict our attention down to a single object, and focus on it. In doing so, we will eliminate the look-alike chambers to a large degree and bring ourselves even closer to that unique chamber which is our intended temporary destination.

Psychics and clairvoyants do this all the time, whether they know it or not. They invoke themselves into chambers without even knowing how they did it or what they're doing; they just follow the motions. They were taught to put a crystal ball in front of themselves, and stare at it until they felt funny, then to start talking. They may fling crushed rose petals all around the room, put a blue or white candle on, wear a particular perfume, put on a certain costume, ring the bell, and so on, but they haven't any of the "why's" and may never come to realize that all this is part of an elaborate shamanistic interdimensional tracking system.

We, on the other hand, try to follow the trail of the Absolute. This is somewhat misleading because anything we find is going to be the Absolute, but of course, once removed, like a second cousin by marriage. We already know that time does not exist in the objective sense, that it is the dim awareness of the next higher spatial dimension which provides the impression of the flow of time. When we traverse any part of the labyrinth, we are always in the after-image, never in the "thing itself".

We might catch a glimpse of the creative radiation itself looking like a revolving beacon coming from the Heart of the Labyrinth scanning around the sphere like a gyroscopic radar sweep, sectioning the crystal-like watery sphere in a shifting sweeping pattern.

The figure is made up of intersectionings of planes; a previous scan is partially broken, then joins another scan as it also breaks the planar sweep.

One could say that the infinity symbol is a cross-section of this structure. It *can* look very much like a sky sweep lighthouse beacon as it sweeps across the chamber illuminating for a moment, and then passing on, but we're never actually in the chamber when it's being formed—we're always in the chamber after it was formed, trailing only a hair's breadth away.

Should we ever actually catch up to the Absolute, we will have to *be* the Absolute, because the Absolute is the Absolute; there can be nothing but the Absolute. No-thing can stand in the face of the Absolute. It all falls; it all becomes absorbed into the Absolute.

Eternity is just a whole lot of now. No later, no then, just lots and lots of now. But that doesn't preclude events! It just means that there's no passage of time except the temporal sensation of the next higher dimension. Not that there is only one passage of the Absolute through Creation.

Eventually, of course, we lose track—it's just another pass through the Creation, and yet it's always the first... We get to the point where we can detect the patterning without the specific arithmetic detail, we are able to determine by rapid non-analytical assessment whether we're breathing in or out at the moment. We always know whether we're at the beginning or the end of an in-breath, the beginning or the end of an out-breath, or the middle. The patterning of breathing seems so self-evident that we find that we can take it for granted.

It's hard for us to comprehend this because we don't have all our faculties at the moment—we're strapped into the Creation, and conversely, we're strapped into the Creation because we don't have all our faculties. If we had all our faculties in the most objective sense, as a higher multi-dimensional being, we would remember exactly how this is all done. It's a very complicated compound equation, but it's built of simplicities. There are only three basic building blocks.

Will, presence and attention; Father, Son and Holy Ghost; affirming, denying and catalytic-reconciling can all serve as names for the building blocks as well as some of the things that the building blocks are made of. Or one, two, three; a, b, c; x, y, and z; Peter, Paul and Mary....

Any three names or designations will do if we understand it to mean that they're the basic building blocks of Creation, elements which, repeated in certain patternings, produce an equation like binary code in one and zero, with which we may be more familiar. Here, however, we are dealing with trinary equations.

Of the three distinct building blocks, each is predicated on the others—there's no first, second and third; they're all equal, each exists only because the others exist. Out of this continuum we can select three other elements in a descending or ascending order, and continue to build from them.

A basic set could be employed to produce a three-dimensional space with one additional temporal level. We can span the space with three perpendicular axes; the orientation of the axis isn't significant in this case, but three radial axes in the same plane are needed to span the space—they needn't be mutually perpendicular.

Behind that, they will be necessarily composed of three basic building blocks which won't change, three basic building blocks which will produce stable mathematical trinities which we can name.

One may even see figurations of four elements or more as building blocks: earth, air, fire, and water is a four-element system, but the system we are interested in is a trinary logic: either / or / and, in which a rider option, a not-necessarily-connected alternative is provided under certain conditions, an auxiliary which can be added without taking away from the first two. Either this, or that, *and* this.

The *and* factor might be zero—*either* this, *or* this, *and* , nothing. The third element may be real or imaginary.

But technical detail will only confuse us and make us hyperactive in the mental. We can know too much for our own good in the sense that we become so enmeshed, so overwhelmed by information, that we lose our perspective on reality. One can have too much detail and perception, especially when the detail runs into the domain of significance, a most annoying ailment which has traditionally afflicted voyagers in every dimension including our own... We can start seeing too much and get caught up and therefore avoid the real issues.

The voyages into the labyrinth are in the larger sense business trips. A certain amount of playfulness may arise in the course of events which would be safe and desirable and productive, but where it isn't, we must make certain that we don't get too playful when we can't afford to . . . One can have a certain amount of pleasure on a business trip, but it should never be at the expense of business . . . .

It all refers back to attention. We've lost attention on where we are and what we're doing, in which case, our habitual assumptions—of who we are, where we are, and what we're doing—will tend to color our every move. The potential for destructive impact that this can have is immeasurable.

If we assume that we are in the human sector, in our human character, with our human characteristics, it's because we've lost attention on the fact that we're voyaging in much higher dimensions. An important part of the business of voyaging is to remember that we're not voyaging for pleasure—although we're certainly going to want to play where we can, and we ought to lack the artificial primate inhibitions which would or could prevent us from playing exuberantly whenever we get a chance to.

In child-birthing, we can't do anything during contractions except work to get the baby out. But between contractions we must use the opportunity to rest as much as we can.

We'll find the same thing in terminus; we experience contractions in leaving the biological machine's electrical field, and we must use those contractions, but then, between the contractions, use these periods for rest.

The malaprop works when he should play, and plays when he should work, thus committing a series of blunders, sometimes expensive. When a malaprop participates in a voyage, it is certain that the voyage won't go anywhere that wouldn't be completely safe even for a malaprop to blunder around in. The presence of malaprops in any embarkation is a very sensitive issue, except, of course, to the malaprop.

**Welcome back to earth,
Fasten safety belts and
Please extinguish all lights.**

E.J. GOLD, *THE WAY IS CLEAR,* OIL, 36''x 48'', 1987.

CHAPTER 15

Going Macrodimensional

Often when we think that we are at our best, we are at our worst, and when we believe we're at our worst, we are at our best, but we can be assured that if we are in the macrodimensions with presence and attention, always and automatically our functioning in the Work chamber conforms to law; we cannot help but be correct.

Voyaging through the labyrinth; a perilous journey at best, not for the diversion and amusement of the idle rich or the busy poor . . . .

The competent voyager gradually becomes aware of subtle signals beckoning us to venture into dangerous dimensions.

These macrodimensions can feel so strange, so foreign, so terrifying; we might be left with the distinct impression that we have been here before, that we know this place; an eerie impression of "déjà vu" in which visual elements, sensory experiences and all-encompassing cognitions awaken deep memories of a dim and primal past. The familiarity is vague, disturbing, misleading.

We may occasionally glimpse macrodimensional reality in our ordinary lives; somehow, accidentally, the perceptual

limits expand and we see more than we think we ought
to . . . .

Creation: a multi-dimensional eternal omnipresent,
pulsating layer upon layer of worlds connected by a soft,
curved complex webwork of pathways—and at the same time
forming isolated self-encapsulating cells of fundamental
notes, periodic crystallization, in which a voyager can easily
become disoriented and temporarily, though eternally,
entrapped and confined.

The world of human primates, far below the Absolute
macrodimension, near the bottom of the shattered fractioning of space and time . . . yet the creatures who inhabit
this world occupy a unique position in the whole of Creation.

Humans: a strange breed of lower primates who, by
some twist of circumstance, possess the potential—seldom
developed—but not necessarily the ability or inclination, to
perform higher dimensional functions, cross-dimensional
voyaging capabilities open to very few beings throughout the
whole of Creation, even though perhaps closer to the
Absolute and more evolved.

The unnatural inclination to use such skills for an
impersonal benefit, like all adult tastes, requires nurturing
and cultivation. Humans could, if they would, develop the
ability to voyage easily through the labyrinth and pass
portals into chambers where others cannot go.

Macrodimensional beings, for all their vast perceptions, clarity and effulgence, cannot access the unobstructed
universe because, while they may perform their own unique
generative functions faultlessly, providing a steady-state
configuration and all necessary activity to achieve flow and
stabilization within their own unique dimensional matrix, the
topological laws governing their existence do not permit
them the freedom to exit this matrix since, unlike the human
primate who corresponds to a superfluous form of viral or
bacterial planetary infestation, they are a profoundly integral
component of their home dimension.

The neophyte voyager should expect to discover with
surprise that the labyrinth conforms not to our predisposi-

tions; disturbing or amusing we may find it, but accommodating, always.

The linear primate mind can grasp only a narrow-band spectrum of Creation and, when confronted with a greater vista, recoils into the rejective anthropomorphic anonymity of the herd.

What a pity that, just when we are most satisfied that, at last, we have a solid grip on one level of reality, it slips through our fingers like a slimy wet fish, which seems to be as graspable as it ever gets . . . .

Are we then to abandon all efforts to mentally order our cosmic-scale experience of the labyrinth? Given the inexorable power of biological life, how can we expect otherwise than to repeat the same primate-level fixations which have kept us comfortably unsatiated in the lower dimensions throughout our lives?

The labyrinth, as any self-respecting shaman will freely admit, is composed—in the musical sense also, as it conforms to the mathematics of the sound, heat, light and rare earths portions of the electromagnetic spectrum—of various matrix formations which can be divided artificially for easy voyage-management into sectors, chambers, corridors and dimensional levels in accordance with our special technical language.

We may decide to quickly dump out—a technical term for a panic-struck retreat—should we become hopelessly disoriented and confused in the trackless wasteland of the labyrinth.

We might have a similar response when we encounter a dead-end, a highly dangerous sector, a zone for which we are not psychologically toughened, emotionally tempered, experience-hardened or simply equipped to handle.

It is with a light heart but not a featherweight brain that a group of voyagers may undertake a labyrinth experiment in the company of experienced and trustworthy voyagers who can play the role of guides in the event that something totally unexpected and potentially disastrous should present itself.

We should keep in mind that macrodimensional residents are not necessarily favorably inclined toward voyagers; for that matter, it is safe to say that we exist for most of them in much the same way as plankton exist in the general attention of a whale.

We are inconsequential creatures in anyone's view but our own. We should keep a perspective on this and realize that the dangers we are facing seldom suggest any more hostility than a leather-soled boot in relation to a cockroach.

Is there a particular type of behavior that is always desirable or advisable in the labyrinth, something to which we might safely resort?

It would be most unwise...unsound...inadvisable—actually, blatantly stupid comes more to mind—to assume that one totally predictable set of rules would apply unilaterally throughout the whole of it. What is appropriate in one space can be quite inappropriate in another.

Danger can visit in many forms, not necessarily conforming to our presumptions. We may be seduced or repelled; fascinated or frightened; devoured or regurgitated; possessed or destroyed; accidentally obliterated or whimsically annoyed, teased, tickled or tamed...and who can guess the real consequences of any of these events and our voluntary and involuntary reactions to them in non-human domains? ....

An artifact—which we define as an accidentally occurring or intentionally and artificially constructed model of a higher or lower dimensional configuration which corresponds in greater or lesser topological exactitude, point-for-point—can provide access to other dimensional levels.

Using an artifact as a guide, an advance scout team—perhaps a few experienced or inexperienced but typicality-appropriate voyagers—can commence exploratory work in the targeted zones.

An appropriate scouting team is composed of the right combination of typicalities—an effective combination, and the word "effective" is the operant factor here, capable of producing an exact result in the macrodimensions, or able to access certain chambers which then act as stepping stones to other macrodimensional chambers.

Effective combinations of typicalities also refer to macrodimensional beings and to the dimensions which they inhabit. Access to macrodimensional beings may require a psycho-emotionally and electrical-field-bonded-cluster of specific typicalities to achieve coalescence. The number of individuals participating in an experimental macrodimensional upscale determines the targeted chamber in conjunction with artifact correspondings which conform to the laws of resonance, and morphological correspondings which conform to the laws of topology.

When a small but effective group of voyagers successfully traverses a difficult sector of the labyrinth, team effort determines how well the group does even if each individual member can't do what others can do.

There will always be a need for individual high-level high-performance quarterbacks, while others will be expected to maintain a quality support team upon which they can unquestionably depend.

The team acts to share the living waking state on the macrodimensional level which, when shared equally rather than left to one, makes work possible.

The diversity of macrodimensional chambers is unlimited both in external and internal aspects: mood, aroma, lighting, ambience, texture... Each voyager will have a unique way of presenting to, and functioning in, the macrodimensional state and its unique and disturbing sensations according to training, typicality, and expendability, a subject we generally avoid.

Fastening our psycho-emotional seatbelts and abandoning the safety and comfort of the primate level, we might find ourselves swamped and barely able to move within a dense, heavy electrical field, and then, just as suddenly, the atmosphere changes; we are struck by a cold, chilling dampness coming from seemingly nowhere ....

A moment later, we find ourselves surrounded by familiar landscapes dissolving not quite so gradually as we'd like, into endless, mysterious intertwining caverns reaching into an unfathomable depth of distant darkness.

While the chambers themselves have some objective existence in the fact that they are crystallizations of fundamental notes within periodically recurring fundamental chords obeying the laws of harmonics, our perception of them is entirely or almost entirely subjective; even so, they can be classified, albeit artificially, by comparative plasticity, electrical density, resistance to movement, effects of color and light, sound reverberation, distortion patterns, degree of connectivity and reciprocity of objects and observers, presence or absence of spatial and communication impedance, and predominant moods, all measured against a single, known and well-examined standard which we have developed in our preparatory work prior to serious labyrinth voyaging which, of course, does not preclude our early exploratory and experimental voyages which are unavoidably steeped in ignorance and imaginative fictionings and, with this in mind, restricted to small and tentative ventures into the uncharted wilderness of nearby macrodimensions.

The mood of one chamber not far removed from the human primate world, and one well-explored by even very ill-schooled primitive shamen of post-Sumerian fame, might best be described by the phrase, "By golly, I *am* my brother's keeper!" (We may see here a vague similarity with certain Old and New Testament reports of this macrodimensional cognition, with the notable absence of the higher mental formulation, "by golly").

In this dimensional level, co-voyaging shamen must— by strict obedience, in the involuntarily conforming sense of a willow bending to the wind—be responsible for one another, acting as personifications of the mood of obligation which characterizes the reflective state in its most manifested form.

A wide variety of exalted moods characterize macrodimensional chambers, numbering in the low zillions, and each mood encountered has its uniquely recognizable smell, taste, and coloration.

In these tentative explorations, the visual elements we encounter are intimately related to the experiential emotional kaleidoscope within ourselves.

Therefore, while we are bound hand, foot and mouth to our primate habits and conditioning, the normal—although a nonprimate outside observer would probably classify it as clinically treatable, running to certifiably committable—range of emotions with which we are familiar is blissfully limited (in the existential-sarcastic view of a Marquis de Sartre) and, with a minimum of educational training, we are able to automatically mistake a grim palette of grays that range from dull to duller to dullest, to the very dullest, to the dullest possible, to unbelievably, incredibly dull, to so damn dull it's all-but-unimaginable, to dull-beyond-dim, to so dull it's downright indistinguishable from bleak, for the dazzling array of possible real emotions emanating from the essential self.

Human primates, in strict deference to their Neanderthal heritage, dwell in wet, shallow cliffside caves of negative body-reactions masquerading as emotions, never guessing at their dwarfed stature.

As primates, we have been trained to restrict our emotional responses to a narrow sandbox-level band within the totality of wide-spectrum hues and colorations of mood which, if we could allow them, would provide us with instantly accessible keys to macrodimensional labyrinthine chambers.

If we were free of primate limitations, even if only the laundromat-centered, daytime soap-opera engendered emotional limitations of the human primate, we would find ourselves able to experience vast, unimaginable emotional heights and depths, most of which even the above-average primate would consider completely intolerable, a searing, seething, screaming Hell created by the flames of unbearable emotional intensity.

Mathematically constructed music provides us with an infinite number of combinations of tempo, flow, rhythm, beat, scale, coloration, oscillation, frequency-sweeps, waveform impactions and a myriad of other effects.

Formatted sound waves—which we call music but which extend far beyond the primate acceptance-level of music—can evoke corresponding mental-emotional excursions within ourselves, occasionally carrying us over into subtle and delicately balanced emotional fugues which because of their utter refinement are germane only to the higher and could not possibly survive in the murky, tonic-destroying atmospheres of the lower dimensions, and which, perhaps in spite of ourselves, dissolve our self-imposed limits, enabling the attention to expand into the macrodimensional levels.

Like all rarefied elements, higher emotions can sometimes be generated by formatted sound in the form of music and other plastic media, and may, whether we are in an allowing mood or not, help us to transcend that part of ourselves which remains dependent on the not-so-late neolithic bone-banging concepts of contemporary human civilization leaning heavily as they do upon the musical doilies of the Baroque.

A chamber which in a lower level remains hardedged and solid, unfolds and softens like an expanding gas in heat as it spirals through an unstoppable escalation into the macrodimensional . . . the shaman rides the crest of this electromagnetic wave . . . the higher chamber is contacted, entered and observed.

The ritual, materials, objects and lingering habits of superstition can all be dispensed with and yet we will have everything really necessary, including without fail a quantity sufficient of that puckish prankstering which magically opens the most resisting doors, for any possible variation in our shamanic meandering, not in the Milesian sense, but meandering with strength, intention and purpose.

Ritual, in this context, can be defined, however questionably, as the enactment or re-enactment—an intentional dramatization—of exact activities encompassing the whole totality of events occurring in a macrodimensional chamber, something like the relationship of early Athenian theatre to events on that dimensional level to which the

Hellenic and preHellenic dramatists referred as "Mount Olympus", having less to do with the oversized hill of the same name and more to do with the interaction of characters in a macrodimension so inconceivable to the primate mind that, when it was encountered by drug-inspired oracular priestesses, they had only the symbolism of earthbound heights from which to draw.

During an average professional macrodimensional voyage, the more experienced situational diagnostician ought to be able to easily identify, correctly mimic and deftly assume the form of any of the resident presences in a higher dimension always unbrokenly in character, never once reacting against the natural flow to reveal one's presence in the macrodimensional form. Form-assumptions should in general remain gently and unaggressively covert unless dictated otherwise by seriously considered necessity when no alternative options present themselves.

Only those forms already eternally existing within a macrodimensional chamber are able to exist in the chamber. The activities and dramas of such inhabitants are unalterable by any means, however powerful, and, knowing this and having a good idea of the inevitable course of such events, a clever voyager can just slip into something uncomfortable—like a macrodimensional form—and, if the voyager's presence does not disturb the occupants of the chamber, observation, learning, communication and exchange are then possible. Therefore, the more exactly the post in the work-drama is mimicked, the more exactly the voyager will resonate with the chamber.

Macrochambers can be compared to rooms in a mansion—not an altogether unfamiliar metaphor to literalist biblical fundamentalists of the worst part of the Western hemisphere, meaning New York, Hollywood, Iowa and their immediate environs—each room representing an individual cosmos isolated from all others by its place in the reality spectrum, from which one may ascend or descend to other dimensions, each of which, for the purposes of this structurization, can be considered a self-contained universe, and from which one may exit laterally into corridors and passages, leading to many similar chambers on the same dimensional level, differing only in their configuration and content.

The labyrinth can be likened to an enormous creature, in each cell of which one or more macrodimensional being resides, unable to leave its own cell. Only a shamanic voyager, being nonphenomenal and having no intrinsic place as part of a dimensional construct, is able to enter or leave the chamber via the voyaging mode.

When we first encounter macrochambers and their macroinhabitants, even though their general form may seem familiar to us, as they resemble our own forms somewhat, because we will tend to voyage into only those chambers within which a corresponding configuration to our usual organic configuration exists, we will probably fail to recognize the transition from the primate into the macrodimensional.

At one end of the scale, we may unaccountably feel a profound sense of undefinable fear, and then, at the other end of the scale, a profound sense of wonder, of awesome beauty . . . or both at once, and then, equally unaccountably, nothing at all.

At yet another point, we may be swept into the presence of what we take to be a single creature of concerted action and intelligence but, should we respond to this clustered being as if it were of singular mood and purpose, we could be committing a dreadful blunder, because as we will soon discover, many macroinhabitants are actually multicellular creatures like the Portuguese man-of-war and the venerable slime-mold, a composite creature which gives the impression of organized consciousness when it shouldn't; an easy mistake from the viewpoint of casual behavioral observation, as one could understandably also conclude in a superficial five-minute study of human primates.

It might help to know that, unaccountably, the central nucleus of a chamber will tend to shift suddenly, perhaps becoming smaller at the core and larger around the circumference, fragmenting in a slow, leisurely disintegration into smaller and smaller units, each of which, despite our subtle, heart-pounding urgings to the contrary, decides to exude multiple appendages and then goes and does it without so much as a by-your-leave, assuming a form just ever so slightly more offensive; this is not a signal to reach for the bottle of tranquilizers; these natural chamber reactions to the impact of our presently crude presences should be perfectly understandable and forgivable to the truly sophisticated voyager.

It might, on the other hand, be disquieting to the organized mind to realize that no two voyages through the labyrinth will ever be exactly the same; one voyage might seem dull and uneventful in comparison to another from which we return in psychoemotional shreds, but from the objective view, they're all the same, except for what happens and to whom.

The facial masks of each of the voyagers can, if not too distorted into bizarre forms of grimace by involuntary reactions to macrodimensional events, provide the means to exit and enter a chamber and, in any case, subjective primate interpretations of macroevents will fall far short of the actual disaster.

Machine manifestations should be treated with the utmost discretion and attention. The experienced shaman takes care not to impinge upon events proceeding in the chamber, especially during a contemplative period of stillness and silence while temporarily inhabiting the form, identity, memory and awareness of one of its macroinhabitants.

The feeling of danger and fear of permanent entrapment—being stuck in a macroreality for what feels like forever—is ever-present. We want to learn to recognize traps and to work within them and pass from them as required by our work. The danger of traps increases as we fall into fascination, distraction, and seduction.

We tend to downscale into lower dimensions as we are drawn by our actions and attitudes into the corresponding events; because we participate actively in them, we are sucked down, reabsorbed into the appropriate lower dimensions, our self-perceptions determining where—in the aftermath of our unceremonious ejection from the macro-dimensional chamber—we find ourselves explosively propelled and unceremoniously deposited.

The panorama of possible macroperceptions and macrosensations is virtually inexhaustible, and most of them will be disturbingly unfamiliar, wrenchingly disorienting and horribly distasteful, but we shouldn't let a little excruciating discomfort inhibit our reckless, indomitable, zestful shamanic self-abandon.

You might as well know right now that some states of confusion are bound to arise at certain predictable periods during any serious incursion into the labyrinth; this is only a reflection of the voyager's predisposition toward the chronic sleeping-state; subjectivity enters when we decide that we are not functioning correctly, when we don't understand the process of self-cleansing automatically caused by the raw radiations to which we are inevitably exposed in any macrodimensional environment.

It may be quite correct to remain, for the moment, entirely ignorant; it is only with long experience that we are able to decide if we should be responding differently to the situation; we might very well consider our functioning inappropriate, throwing ourselves wholeheartedly into the more familiar primate reactions; remorse, guilt, fear, shame, paranoia, and other self-produced imaginative subjective reactions, but in a work chamber we cannot do otherwise than function correctly, because, at the moment, *we are not ourselves,* but we *are* responsible for our continued presence.

All events in a macrochamber are part of the construction of the chamber; what appear to us as linear, connected temporal events over which we have control and within which we ought to be able to exercise our personal will on an immediate experiential dimensional level can be perceived from the next-higher dimensional level as an integral and inalterable part of the whole configuration.

Ironically, we have the greatest resistance to our own correct functioning and the more correct the functioning, the more stupid we feel, the more glaringly we feel ourselves standing out in the crowd, the only one who isn't able to see and understand what's going on, what needs to be accomplished, the one who always asks all the stupid questions, but the fact is, everyone in a chamber has the same opinion, except the local macroinhabitants, of course.

If we're not too steeped in the human primate reality, and not too intrusive to stop the flow of macrodimensional activity, we might notice the unique interactions between macroinhabitants of the chamber.

We might participate in the re-unification of macro-beings, prime fracturings of the Absolute, who have taken the form of interflowing male and female aspects sandwiched on either side of an intermediary plasma float, reaching out toward one another in an energy-enforced illusion of separation; as the macrobeings close the gap between themselves, the plasma becomes noticeably more dense, at last unbearably so, just short of actual contact.

We may find our host macrobeings bypassing Creation, working directly together to achieve the same goal of total contact, at the same moment discovering once again to their utter dismay that one is all alone . . . all one.

We may perhaps even become dimly aware that our group of voyagers is being covertly scrutinized—and evidently graded on a bell-curve—by someone or something about which we'll eventually be forced to know more; or we may be thunderstruck with the sudden illumination that, *here we actually are*, in the midst of an excursion into the unknown, a very long way from home.

> **It's always
> The insignificant
> Little things
> That turn out to be
> The master Keys.**

CHAPTER 16

Life in the Labyrinth

We work to overcome our fears of seeing the horror of the situation and to achieve the Heart of the Labyrinth where we are able to perform a special kind of work, view the Creation as a whole, and put life into it, if only momentarily.

All creatures great and small in the animal kingdom have natural enemies that they can *see, sense, smell* and identify directly. Human beings, on the other hand, have only one natural enemy—an enemy that they can't see, can't sense, can't smell, and only have a vague idea about.

Human animals, being of the more elaborately mentally equipped—but not a truly intelligent species—creatures of the primate persuasion, deal with their fear of this, their only non-imaginary natural enemy by turning it into something romantic. But there is nothing romantic or imaginary about this enemy; the fact of the matter is—*a human primate's only natural enemy is the Absolute.*

This idea can be better appreciated if we understand that human beings are, in a very fathomable way, useful to the Absolute—but only when they've graduated from the claustrophobic kindergarten world of the human primate.

Our whole relation with the Absolute can best be summed up with the idea that *the Absolute is in pursuit of human beings* and that the primary occupation and majority of energy expenditure of human beings seems to be dedicated almost entirely toward protecting themselves from the Absolute. All our involvements, pursuits, pleasures and pains are protective projections and buffers, which serve as barriers between ourselves and the Absolute. It could be said that *the whole of life is a struggle against eternity.* This catastrophic primate struggle is a clear demonstration of our flight from the Absolute and from the macrodimensional worlds which the Absolute has left in its immediate wake.

In a very real way, we've deliberately lost ourselves in the lowest levels of the labyrinth, immersed in the trivial pursuits of human primate life, which effectively bars us from exposure to the Absolute or, for that matter, from anything which lies even a little beyond the primate world.

Understanding in what way time does not exist enables us to grasp the idea that the Absolute is not in a hurry to get results out of the Creation.

The Absolute, being free of time and space, isn't working against a deadline, and so impatience is not an aspect of the Absolute. Anxiety, possibly; gnawing preoccupation, less probably; but certainly not pressed for time.

If macrodimensional beings have learned anything at all about the Creation, it's that instilling life into the Creation can't be rushed any more than a loaf of bread or a good bowel movement.

Macrodimensional beings aren't going anywhere and have nowhere to go; on their level of existence, there's not enough mass-energy stuff out there to give them any place to go; it's all contained within the chamber they happen to occupy.

But we—we *do* have places to go, things to do, people to see—us humans have such important business to conduct; such vital primate games to play, such necessities to buy . . . so many department stores and so little time!

We ought to feel pity for macrodimensional beings who have nowhere to hide and nothing to do, other than their objective work within their eternalized chambers, and certainly nothing to buy... unless, of course, their eternalized chamber happens to resemble a department store.

We could describe our deep and unbreakable obsession with primate life as a game of "Hide and Seek" — heavily loaded on the side of hiding and mighty slim on the seek side—in which we skillfully avoid all contact with the whole uncomfortable question of macrodimensional reality.

It is in the macrodimensional that we will learn to perform the Work, that we will inch our way closer and closer to the heart of the problem and also at the same time toward the very heart of the Work.

And so we must have the courage to explore beyond our self-imposed human primate limitations, and open ourselves up to the silent cry that beckons us from within, that haunts us to the core, and that has always been our inner guide through the dark oppressive passageways behind us and which lie still ahead of us an uncountable and unguessable distance.

If we are to work in the macrodimensional sectors of the labyrinth, we must study the Work as it is, not as we imagine it to be, and study the methods of Work as they are and not as we would perhaps prefer. We could impose our existing beliefs and habits on the Work, but then we mustn't expect to really perform work.

It is foolish—stupid, actually would be a more choice description—to assume that, just because we have some vague noble aspiration and ambition to change something because we're bored or tired or upset with the way things are, or we have a gnawing urge to leave our crude personal graffiti somewhere very visible, or out of an acquired sense of cinematic heroism, we are automatically endowed with the ability to do so.

Ability is dependent upon inner attitudes, natural aptitudes, and the most powerful of all disciplines, the ability to defer gratification. It is also somewhat dependent upon circumstance and chance . . . about ninety percent.

In the long process of approaching the work of the macrodimensional shaman—a realistic goal we can set for ourselves, but which we must come to recognize will require years and even decades of serious preparation—we will require of ourselves the will and attention of the essential self applied in very freely adapted but strictly methodical ways, guided by common sense, strong discipline, and the kind of deep respect for the higher dimensions that an electrician develops for 240 volt power supplies.

Ultimately, it furthers the superior shaman to learn how to get along without all those standard primate imperatives so dear to the hearts of not-quite-as-hairless-as-they'd-like-to-believe apes of the human variety.

We will devote thousands of hours to repeated practice in an invocational circle, and eventually come to realize that we must deal rather rapidly with our most fang-baring fears of the macrodimensional world, and progressively adjust ourselves in a way that will lead us face-to-face with . . . what?

This distinctly paradoxical source of attraction and repulsion has throughout our lives consistently produced a mildly obsessive gut-level gnawing within us; happily, we at least now know its cause, if not its cure.

The intelligent labyrinth voyager is constrained by artificially induced habit to see and to know with clarity and lucidity, to feel with full intensity, to function effectively, to respond elegantly, which is to say, minus those primitive pursuits and superstitions which keep the primate self so bound up in negative emotional knots.

The disciplined shaman is expected to remain relaxed and calm while exposed to the full impact of macrodimensional reality. Reality . . . a hell of a dirty trick to play on an unsuspecting voyager . . . .

The first degree of shamanistic proficiency is attained when we are able to perform the exercise of Objective Prayer or Prayer-Absolute.

The initial mood of Prayer-Absolute, as we attempt to raise the dead in the original New Testament sense, which is to say, to bring the corpse of the Creation to life, is very close to an almost intolerably intense emotional state of abject horror and involuntary loathing at being apparently permanently attached as a kind of Siamese twin—in an eternal state of existence, mind you—to an enormous, cadaverous thing on an unimaginable scale, combined with a feeling of impending doom intermixed with liberal doses of total, fatalistic inescapability.

As we open ourselves emotionally and perceptually, revealing to ourselves this saddening vision which the Tibetans have been trying to sell us for years, we will inevitably experience a wrenching feeling of repulsion rising from the very depths of our innermost stillness, becoming more and more unbearable, which the Tibetans consider great fun.

If we are able to remain neither attracted nor repelled, we will then enter a subjective state as if struck dumb with fear and terror; but we must agree to temporarily remain unmoved and unresisting in the midst of our terror without dwelling too much on the overwhelming aspect of this confrontation. A feeling of helplessness—we cannot directly assist by providing the force or initiative toward the waking state—and of deep, despairing hope, will soon sink in . . . .

We may then passingly note the mood of irony at the sheer *eternity-ness* of it all, when we suddenly realize, perhaps for the first time, that it really *isn't* ever going to end, and that there *is* no real escape outside the subjective dreamstate of the lower dimensions . . . .

As we feel the sensations of horror, as the reality of eternal affixment to a floating corpse supported by some unknowably immense high-density electromagnetic field sinks in, with our perception as keen, vivid and intense as it has ever been, we capture a crystal-clear vision of the all-embracing immensity of the corpse of Creation, and as we do so, the necessity, shamanistically speaking, to fight the automatic urge to blur the vision, and instead focus clearly, closely and lovingly at every detail of this lifeless, yet animated—even erotic—cadaver, may suggest itself.

If we understand clearly the method of Prayer-Absolute—and most of us won't—we will draw our cosmic necrophilous lover more and more deeply toward ourselves, enfolding it with breathless love and the totality of our attention, taking the utmost care not to accidentally or unknowingly inflict our own life-force into it . . . If it is to live, it must come to life on its own initiation . . . .

Holding all this in balance . . . and the paradox may trouble us deeply . . . at the correct moment, we intentionally, suddenly, gasp in an instantaneous blend of joyous surprise and abject horror, eyes agape . . . pun very intentional . . . and in the moment of this gasping surprise, if our timing is exactly right, our vision will suddenly and automatically adjust itself; we will, for a fleeting moment— so brief as to have an air of unreality to it, and yet so real as to have a taste of eternity—catch a glimpse of the Absolute, outlined and illumined in a nimbus of brilliant radiation, almost invisible, which flashes and is gone as instantly as it appears.

In this act, *the Absolute is seen and known.* The truth, clarity and force of this experience will leave a permanent scar across the mind, and an insatiable yearning in the being.

The performance of this special sharp inbreath is derived from ancient Greek practices at Delphi. The Greeks had a word for it; we today call it "the Classical Gasp".

Prayer-Absolute is not prayer toward the Absolute, it is the descending incantation of the Absolute itself, roughly equivalent to the thought, *Oy, oy, somebody get me down from here . . . hurry . . . I can't hold out much longer!*

The shocking inbreath of the Classical Gasp causes a reverberation within us—an electrical tingle which overtakes us as recognition dawns upon us, and allows us to instantaneously transform ourselves into living lightning rods for the descent of the Absolute toward ourselves and, through us, down the totem, the progression of descending macrodimensional formations from the highest to the lowest crystalline mineral world, surprisingly, the least dense, having the least amount of mass-energy contained in its nucleic chambers and the greatest mass-energy density in its surrounding environment—near which we find the world containing human primates busily engaged in wiping out any genuinely intelligent life forms such as the dolphin, the eggplant, and the tomato.

In our shamanistic functioning as lightning rods, we provide the electrical and topological connectivity; a totem of simultaneously ascending and descending dimensional forms from the lowest to the highest dimensional level and therefore, because we occupy the entire totem, we are the totem as a whole, and can feel and sense this as it occurs.

This sensation and its resulting emotional mood is just one of the subjective penalties we pay during the performance of Prayer-Absolute, but it is as necessary to have available to us the sensations of our action as it is for the human primate to have available the sensations of the skin, for example, without which movement—and even basic survival—would be chancy, which means, "not bloody likely".

In our performance of Prayer-Absolute, we must bring ourselves into the posture, subjective mood and cognitive position of the Absolute—suggested by sculptural representations of the Man on the Cross, but which we have just glimpsed in its reality—maintaining this in stillness and in silence as long as we can possibly tolerate it, at least to a slow count of 24, timed to a full, sonorous cycle of inbreath and outbreath, corresponding to a full creation cycle regulated by the "breathing"—if it can be called that, and it often is—of the Absolute.

It might be interesting to note that what human primates might call "davening"—a rhythmic rocking motion in time to silent or verbal intonation of sacred chanting—or "lovemaking" is, on the highest dimensional level, "breathing".

The flow of apparent location of the Observing Absolute within this unicellular—but obviously nearly completely mitotic—organism determines the duration of breathing cycles, passing from the non-existent absence of all attributes, the Absolute, to and through the presence of all possible attributes, the Creation, and back again.

The experience-grizzled shaman will find no surprise in the fact that a voyager in a particularly primate frame of mind will be unable to maintain this state for more than one or two full breathing cycles, which is to say, a count of one or two billion subjective millenia or seconds, whichever seems longer.

When we can't hold out any longer, we needn't worry; another shaman, refreshed from a short vacation on one or another of the lower worlds, will probably wander nonchalantly along . . . just as we did . . . and slowly taking notice of our distress, will offer in a slow drawl—as sweat, metaphorically speaking, gushes down our macrodimensional brow—to take our place; of course, always far too slowly and, for our taste, just a hair too late . . . .

As we lose our sweaty macrodimensional grip on the Absolute a split-moment before our relief shaman takes hold, we note *en passant*—which in this case means "on the way down"—the chilling fact that very few beings are willing... and able . . . to perform this intensely impersonal sacrifice.

It provides no comfort to know that every living being will, completely involuntarily, perform a single moment of this sacrifice during that millisecond in the process of organic death when the essential self and the biological machine are terminally wrenched apart.

A hell of a lot of good that does! Might as well not bother at all. Now, if only there were more individuals willing to voluntarily assume the Cross . . . but, of course, they never have been, aren't now, and most likely, if all eternity is any indication, never will be, then things would be different, which they aren't.

At this point, we are ready to assume the position, as they say, and to view the Creation from the viewpoint of the Absolute.

Now we have a different problem. It's expected of a shaman at this point to perform Objective Prayer, which is very different from Prayer-Absolute which, you will recall, is the assumption of the posture of the Absolute for your basic 24 count or bust.

Objective Prayer, on the other hand, is the attempt to use the directed forces of love—in the objective sense—and the attention of the essential self to help the Creation bring itself to life, momentarily or best offer.

In every labyrinth voyage we undertake, (and here we must pause to consider the necrotic condition of the Creation) we are forced inevitably to pass through the Heart of the Labyrinth, the central gateway to all macrodimensional chambers and as we do so, we must not neglect one part of our work, to bring transforming catalysts to various macrodimensional beings of a slightly lower order, trapped eternally in a single, generally unbelievably boring, cosmically bureaucratic work-chamber.

One such catalyst is, "You can't change the situation, but you *can* learn to like it . . . " We are expected to charge about from chamber to chamber as energy and attention allow, delivering this and other similar little nuggets of useful information to the residing and presiding inhabitants.

But for that part of our work in which we act as lightning rods for the descent of the Absolute from the Cross, and then during this assumption, sweat blood, more or less, in our efforts to bring the Creation to life, we depend largely upon our ability to utilize higher emotions, which are exactly those emotions which empowered us to pass easily through the Heart of the Labyrinth on our way to the highest macrodimension.

In a sense, our passage through the Heart of the Labyrinth guarantees that we are able to perform these exalted two forms of palliative macrodimensional work.

Assemblages of shamanically trained voyagers, a single, double, or multiple bonded nucleic cluster (connected apparently, to the casual outside observer, indirectly—as in stage performers, dancers, priest or priestess, invocant or what-have-you—or directly—as in sexual conjunction) surrounded by a living, consciously directed acutely observational periphery—as in a theatre audience in the round, or a congregation in a temple, or a sexual seance with a large number of participants some active, some passive—providing additional force and mass-energy density to the nucleus, enabling the shaman to maintain the Creation in a living state for a much longer period, are able to perform very intense and highly stable forms of Prayer-Absolute and Objective Prayer, but such shamanic assemblies are far more rare than the individual fly-by-night shaman only able to maintain the state for a moment or two; obviously the bonding of ordinarily irreconcilable typicalities is very difficult—nearly impossible without some bloodshed, metaphorically speaking... well, in general, metaphorically.

The key to all this is to be able to assume the posture of the Absolute and then act from that viewpoint; this requires many factors of mood, thought, sensation, perception and reaction quite different from our customary primate state.

A blend of exaltation and horror produce the mood of the Man on the Cross. This balance of extremes, at its most intense, is what we have been both running away from and at the same time looking for, all our lives. It is the goal, knowingly or unknowingly, of every saint living and dead.

The figure of the Man on the Cross is, as we can see by its representation in three dimensions, fixed firmly in place by three nails, the affirming, the denying and the reconciling... father, son, and unseen essential spirit which moves freely within.

Each nail is unreal in the sense that they fixate the form only because the Bearer of the Cross holds them in place: the first, by self-initiated and self-directed attention; the second, by intentionally invoked self-presence; the third, by sheer will, the will to remain on the Cross strictly voluntarily, disregarding the intensity of discomfort and the ease by which one could descend if, for a single moment, one succumbed to the sweet seduction of sleep and relief, our only refuge from eternity.

All this can serve to remind us of our deep yearning for the Beloved, the other face of the Absolute, of which we only capture fleeting glimpses as it skirts around corners, disappearing into the darkness. A glance of the tip of a robe, a heel, a subtle lingering perfume, all of which hint at the incomplete vision we see, and the all-embracing beauty for which we restlessly search.

We are left wondering whether the Beloved is something we have invented to fill our dreams and torment our souls, but in spite of disillusionment and disenchantment, and perhaps *because* we have dispelled the illusions and enchantments which have bound us, we continue undaunted in our quest, utilizing every possible means to seek out the Beloved, only occasionally—generally about three in the morning—giving ourselves up to temporary, but total, despair.

Our dogged perseverance may open up new avenues of pursuit, although if we depend on bulldoggish stubbornness, the outcome is dodgy at best.

The best approach is to apply the trained and disciplined attention as an instrument which can enable us to approach the Beloved; through discipline, we may find ourselves slowly moving from a position of dissatisfaction, distance and incompleteness to a position of proximity— more than sufficient for our life-giving purposes—to the Beloved.

Imagine being attached forever to a dead lover, and suddenly, without warning, finding oneself making love to this grisly, empty creature, knowing all the while that, if it only would, it has the potential to come to life.

Wouldn't we make every possible attempt to bring this lover to life? ... Form a minyan of ten, a decalogue, bowing in motion, lovemaking prayer to coax the Creation, in the form of the Shekinah, to life.

To the Absolute, the Creation is a dead lover, forever and irremovably inseparable—a sight from which the Absolute cannot withdraw its vision.

The shaman, on the other hand, is a member of the privileged view; we can relieve ourselves periodically of the situation and can then gather the strength to act upon it and temporarily repair it.

Should we foolishly choose to devote the remainder of our existence—which could add up to a considerable sum, as in *cogito ergo*—to this Work, we are destined to a horrible fate as cosmic janitors, software experts with the mission to bring the Creation to life.

If we understand that being is a single thing of definite measure, then we will understand that we infuse life by giving up some of our own, but in the form of attention and love.

On the dimensional level where this can take place, being is not fractioned and Creation can be viewed as a dead lover. At this level even above the highest macrodimension, no labyrinth exists; the universe is just an empty sack. Its internal complexity increases only as the dimensional levels decrease by an elaborate fractioning process which follows the laws governing light, sound and other electromagnetic wave and particle phenomena. The infusion process which is initiated in these higher levels is somewhat similar to cellular mitosis.

Fractioning begins immediately following the mitotic process, and once the fractioning begins, the dimensional level on which the infusion took place is no longer maintained against entropy; having once existed it will not cease to exist on this level of macrodimensionality.

The infusion of life-force by mitotic fission of the nucleic inhabitant of each dimension then continues into the lower levels.

Our position of nonparticipant-observer can be utilized in order to verify whether the Creation is still dead or has responded to shamanic stimulation by coming to life.

In the typical scenario, the Creation slowly comes to life, blossoms in sheer breathtaking beauty, a vision of rapturous delight, dancing in brilliant splendor, then we are forced to watch helplessly as it withers, crumples and collapses almost instantly into a dry, wrinkled and horribly shriveled petrified gray lump, like a water-drenched Disney witch or a bargain face-lift gone bad.

If there's a moral to all this, it's probably something like, never assume you know who you're with just because they look like someone you know . . . and were with a moment ago, and who hasn't left the room since you last looked.

Many gateways
That lead
To the Heart of the Labyrinth
Have no human connotations.
The price
Of Absolute intimacy
Is to be alone.

E.J. GOLD, *A BOTTLE OF SPIRITS,* OIL ON CANVAS, 36'' x 48'', 1987.

CHAPTER 17

Bringing Creation to Life

The effort to bring Creation to life is never-ending. At first distant, the actual possibility of performing this task will be achieved again and again during our work in the labyrinth. This talk is a reconstruction of a successful group voyage.

I came into the chamber around midnight feeling quite exhausted. There was a light chatter between the three invocants who seemed to be at an interval and I went more or less unnoticed as I started preparing my bedding.

I realized that E.J. was preparing to voyage and I immediately felt torn between participating or just going into my corner and sleeping; I might have to leave the room if I wanted to sleep . . . I really didn't feel like having a passive role as usual and I wasn't interested in getting upset, knowing that my fatigue was already distorting my reactions and perceptions.

I reluctantly joined the circle at the reluctant urging of those present, fully realizing that I would have to let go of my negativity . . . This turned out to be much easier than I had expected, and we began to go macrodimensional.

From then on, I must admit, my early linear recollections are fuzzy. Time literally stopped, we were in a timeless space, and I have no idea how long we worked or of the order of many of the events. I felt propelled into a series of cycles rather than experiencing a linear sequence of events.

The only reference to time that I remember had to do with what is called, in the human sector, a television set and which served as a communication device with other beings in this chamber. Early on in the voyage it gave us the message "Time is now."

Contrary to my habit of closely observing my surroundings and getting a general overview of the situation, my attention was totally riveted to the nucleus of this particular macrodimension, to the extent that I never lifted my eyes from it, although it did occur to me—at least at one point—to take stock of everything. But I just couldn't bring myself to turn my attention away from what was happening in the center of the chamber. My surroundings simply did not have enough reality to warrant a deviation from my single-pointed intention and attention.

The mood I experienced most of all was of fluidity and smoothness; in a sense, it was as if everything was very relaxed, although this does not really properly describe what I was feeling. It was almost as if I felt that we were sailing, rather than having difficulty or needing to make tremendous efforts to voyage from chamber to chamber.

My senses were not particularly sharpened, although not necessarily dull. Perhaps slightly sluggish without any feeling of heaviness. I had absolutely no sense of time. Everything was at a standstill.

We started out as three and everything felt remarkably smooth to me. E.J. even commented as we made a turn that we had just made a really nice pass, or landing, or something to that effect. He cheered us on and M. added something also—an expression that I was not familiar with. It was as if he was talking to an observer who should take note that we had not only done well but had done more than was required. Anyway it was a good beginning.

It was during this interval that he also said that we needed B. in the chamber, so M. went out to see if she was in the house, but came back saying that she was not . . . B. did come in soon after that though . . . .

I remember early on in the invocation when we were sitting in a circle; E.J. expressed something with such finesse that I felt like clapping and cheering him on. It was a beautiful verbal tour de force that was such a delight to witness. I wanted to include it in *Life in the Labyrinth.* The idea he expressed was that perceptions usually lie in the macrodimensions, whereas sensations can usually be relied upon.

This statement felt utterly momentous to me; I had heard it said a few days earlier, but this time it really struck home. I was thunderstruck, realizing at last the importance of this key to maze brightness.

When we began working in the circle, I had the feeling that I had much to learn from the women here. Whereas I had an ability with the formulation of the ideas in a coherent written form "out there", the women in the chamber—especially when *in* the chamber—had abilities and experience that I was only beginning to glimpse, let alone experience.

I was soon drawn in close, feeling quite compatible with what was occurring—if compatible is a good choice of word.

I've taken to being more calm and hoping that things will work out rather than getting uptight and forcing myself to move in and out of spaces; I've discovered that if I am relaxed then I can ease into spaces, although I do have a certain apprehension that I might be too slow or not intense enough. Nevertheless I proceeded at the pace I felt comfortable with, not rushing into any wildly impressive flourishes.

It was quite delightful and playful! I was reminded of times when we have danced together, openly intimate, and I have felt that we were making love, or have wanted to make love afterwards.

At another point we interacted with the video monitor which provided us with direction and cues. Video clues provided much interaction and quite surprising feedback at several key intervals.

All the while I felt extremely connected to this central nucleus with my total attention fixated on it. In fact, my attention was so connected to it that I couldn't bring myself to turn my attention away—even for a moment. My surroundings were more like a sketchy, intangible cardboard set than anything else; they were not particularly real at that level, already somewhat removed from where I was.

A little later in the voyage, I had the feeling that I must have made a wrong move. We broke and then a conversation between E.J. and the television set ensued which was remarkable in itself. As far as I could understand, questions were being put to E.J. from an outside source, or by observers. The questions themselves seemed to be coming through with some wave interference, but they were very direct, and questions and answers were clearly connected.

One of the questions had to do with one of the participants; they—whoever they were—wanted to know what was going on and if everything was all right; E.J. indicated yes.

This exchange was a very strong moment in the voyage and a good sample of the type of phenomena that characterized it. The interaction with the television set was most astounding to me, and E.J.'s ability to hold a conversation and take his cues from audible input into the space was quite remarkable, even though we all have seen him conversing directly with the television set before; this voyage had a different quality to it as far as this element is concerned and went much further than anything I had ever been conscious of before. Perhaps what was most different from my point of view was that the presence of outside observers had never been so clearly obvious to me.

Several changes then quickly followed in rapid succession. Two voyagers, at various points, were instructed to view the television set as an audiovisual display representing the ongoing workings of their headbrain. It was pointed out to them that the TV would just keep playing in the corner. They were each asked whether they had to actually be, that is, suffuse their identity in, the TV, and each one said "no". And he said, "Fine, we'll continue..." He thanked one of them for letting us see inside her brain. The circle laughed; we all knew her very well, and it was very funny to see how true this was—it really *was* her brain with its tone, interests, and habits!

I was pulled in once more to the nucleus. I remember losing bodily sensation for a while and thinking that I would have to continue voluntarily, and I did with no problem; but it really was because I had decided to, and not at all automatically.

A danger seemed most definitely present. One of us had to take the initiative to break what was happening. It seemed as if we got out of that one smoothly enough, although at another point things seemed a little more rough.

In a different sequence, when I began working actively at the nucleus once again, E.J. instructed me that *I should view the form I saw before me as dead.* He stressed that I must not initiate any reaction or response unless it happened of itself, from its own self-initiation.

E.J. was apparently not satisfied that the directives were clear to me and so repeated what it was he wanted me to do. He asked me if I understood and I acknowledged. I repeated what he said and he said that was exact, and then said we were going to take off—which we immediately did. I would normally have asked a few more questions for precision, but felt that under the circumstances, it would not be appropriate to dally in mental and verbal formulations. So I decided I had better fly by the seat of my pants.

After the voyage, I had the opportunity to ask about this, and expressed the fact that it had been very clear to me that this was extremely serious and that I felt that the consequences of a wrong move would have been enormous.

It had occurred to me that I might be utterly repulsed by the vision of a solid eternally unbreakable connection to a dead lover and had felt inside myself a mild apprehension about the possibility of rejecting what I would see, which I felt would be very wrong. I knew that this was going to be *for real* and that such a *faux-pas* could only be accidental, a result of momentary inattention....

Had I reacted to the vision, and pulled away and rejected it, the Creation—as it was in that dimension—would have shattered and fragmented into the tiniest possible units. This would have been a terrible downscale for it—and myself. Any such reaction would have constituted a *sudden move*—something to avoid at all cost because, as we know, the consequences of actions in macrodimensions reverberate all the way down to the lower.

I went into a relaxed mode, not wanting to initiate anything. I looked at E.J. and he seemed so very different from anything I had ever seen him appear to be before. I didn't know it, but I was going to see many things that I most certainly had never seen before.

The sensing changes were the strongest element throughout the whole voyage. They were subtle but recognizable, definable, and distinctive. I was in the same place, only it wasn't the same place. Nothing new appeared in my perception, but the *quality* of new surroundings—the characters and the dimensionality were very different.

I was struck by the *scale* on which things were taking place. This was not the human level, although this creature in front of me had an identity which I could conveniently assign to it—something familiar on the human level. But here, it was something else. We were on a macro scale. A lot was contained in us and depended on us. E.J. appeared as an enormous creature—enormous, meaning the size of a universe, or more. I could not really guess what he presently incorporated, nor fathom its limits. The enormity I experienced had nothing to do with visual changes, it was strictly qualitative. I experienced the momentum and weight of this scale and guessed at his macrofunction.

I did not feel or see anything particularly striking after that. Perhaps I was too phlegmatic or passive during that passage, in any case it eventually ended, although I do not recall how. I do remember not knowing when I should consider this particular instruction complete, and whether I was supposed to continue in the same mood as instructed earlier, so I maintained the attitude I believed to be appropriate.

I changed places and became once again a passive observer. I remember lying on my side with my full attention once again riveted to the central nucleus, feeling very connected to it. *All of a sudden, out of nowhere I saw what was in front of me as the Creation, and plainly saw that it was dead.* It was as if I was looking at it, seeing it as an ordinary configuration, and then suddenly doing a doubletake, realizing that *it really was dead.* There was no detail to this perception, no added features. It was still the same chamber, same cast of characters, but they were incorporating the totality of Creation and the whole thing was really, really dead. It was truly horrible! Far beyond anything I could ever imagine, because it was real, it wasn't just a thought.

This vision was extremely brief, briefer than my usual insights. It was so intense and clear, however, that I actually gasped, although probably no one else noticed my inbreath or the fact that I started slightly with an involuntary spasm. It was the first time this vision had been so powerfully and convincingly clear to me.

So, on the one hand, it seems as if, when we get to a certain level, we are able to see the horror of the situation and know its reality. The Creation is dead, just as the machine is asleep, only the scale is so grand, so absolutely enormous, that it is a source of horror for us, for itself, and for its progenitor and eternal companion, the Absolute, once removed. The more we look at this dead Creation, the more horrible it becomes, the more overwhelming and frightening.

The realization that the Absolute is, in a sense, really practicing necrophilia, can be thoroughly terrifying, utterly devastating. How can one be prepared to make love to a truly cold, limp dead thing?

In the chamber at the top, where the whole of Creation is visible and quite lifeless, a knowledge of the enormity of what is involved here comes and goes. At once this huge, monstrous creature called Creation, and at the same time a solid entity with no referents to scale but itself; therefore relatively small, from its subjective point of view.

It isn't just the deadness of Creation; it seems filled with a fear of life, just as our human biological machines have the fear of the waking state . . . only, on an unimaginably vast scale. We, as shamanistic voyagers, wish to give Creation *the habit of coming to life,* so that it is no longer so antithetical to it.

The voyage of that particular night was an attempt at bringing the Creation to life. Several attempts were made, much as one strikes flint on steel, over and over again until a spark is generated; then, with the help of gentle, continuous fanning, perhaps a small flame—wavering, hesitant, uncertain—flickers and finally catches for a moment or two . . . The hope is that one day it will *really* take, so that it lasts, although this wonderful flame of life, even though eternal, would not be entirely permanent, because all living things, even on such a scale, must die; life, after all, is breath, and outbreath surely follows inbreath . .

From this point of view, I was told afterward by E.J. himself in response to a direct question, that the voyage was a success. The Creation *did* come to life, even though briefly. I did not see it however; hopefully next time I will not be so blind . . . .

Not all voyages
Are concerned with
Bringing the Creation to life,
But voyages of this type are.

E.J. GOLD, *COSMO STREET CORRIDOR,* OIL, 48''x 36'', 1987.

EPILOGUE

The Force of Attention

Having made several attempts at penetrating the labyrinth, we will return to our starting point, asking ourselves what the shamanic voyager's secret is. The answer is simple — everything depends upon attention. It is a tool which we all possess; the rest is up to us.

If the voyager has recognized these ideas, tasted the eternal, familiar sorrow of the Absolute, and its true relationship to the macrodimensions, then we must be feeling that inconsolable yearning to find and penetrate the Heart of the Labyrinth, at the same time disturbed by the meager results of our previous efforts and the frustration of knowing that we must continue to act, still not knowing quite where to begin.

But we can only work with what we have at the moment; we need only attention, presence and will of attitude. What remains of our primate lives, and what we don't need, is mechanical involvement and occluded attention.

Involvement in primate pursuits is one of our principal obstacles to approaching the Work and seeing where we as voyagers are in the labyrinth as well as where we might be able to go.

Involvement with the outside world, with desires, repulsions, attachments, or the vital interests common to monkeys everywhere is a symptom of our lost and restless wandering, oblivious to the awesome majesty of the macrodimensional labyrinth, as we allow our precious lives to dribble through our fingers like fine sand.

What ordinarily becomes of the attention, our most precious possession? We foolishly spend it on trivia, allowing it to be caught and diverted, accepting the total organic exploitation of our extremely finite work energy.

If only we could learn to protect ourselves from the urgent demands of nature, we would at least cease to allow our higher intentions to be dissipated.

Competent labyrinth voyaging depends upon the ability to develop attention, and from the platform of waking-state skills, to move out of the primate morphology into unfamiliar macromorphologies compatible with the Work.

Along these lines, we will begin ruthlessly evaluating everything which purports to be *important* and making uncompromising value judgments about our attention on a minute-to-minute basis. We may eventually be able to resist the pressure of lower dimensional intrusions, and begin to see them as mere reflections of our profound state of sleep and occlusion.

We begin to perceive the devastating influence of primate pursuits, ripping the attention away from the macrodimensional perspective; it is the mechanism which inevitably forces us to descend involuntarily into the lower human sector preoccupations.

Attention motivated by a low-grade biological machine hunger indicates a definite lack of understanding of the most basic labyrinthine discipline, and of the fundamental demands of Work.

We must first find the attention of the essential self, and then develop the will to place, withdraw, re-place,

196

expand and concentrate the attention, to put it where we want it, and make it stick, without intrusions, for as long as we wish it to remain. Without this first ability, we have no platform from which to hope for any serious work in the macrodimensions.

Simple loss of attention in which the attention has not been attracted or ripped away by an outside intrusive force, but wanders on its own accord is directly tied to the fact that the essential self is not normally the source of attention, and that the machine is easily bored and distracted.

All forms of attention—mental, emotional, and physical—can be retrieved and replaced elsewhere as we would place a stone or chesspiece on a gameboard; for example, we can voluntarily place our emotional attention, our heart, as we choose, just because we decide to direct in this way and have through our preparatory work developed the will as one develops the strength and skill of coordination in the eye and the hand.

If attention fails, it means either that the essential self is not producing presence and attention because it has been distracted, or that something has broken the attention, perhaps even violently.

Should we seriously try to develop the three voluntary skills; presence, attention and attitude, inevitably we will notice some interruptive, distracting and intrusive elements; some more strident and insistent than others.

Persisting in our efforts, we will begin to notice with great irony a category of subtleties which may have eluded us in our early work, things of no consequence *which we have always dismissed as irrelevant,* and which we have consistently failed to recognize as responsible for capturing and severely impinging upon our attention, even the attention of the essential self, such as it is at present.

The most seemingly harmless and insignificant reactions which arise in ourselves, or events which arise in our surroundings and pull us away from even our most firm purposes and intentions are those very things we should be most on guard against, because they are so insignificant as to penetrate the defenses of our attention; so small as to easily bypass the immunity-screen of self-knowledge; involuntary interruptions of the attention are symptomatic of a blind spot in ourselves. If we saw what distracts us, we might not be so easily seduced into the trivial and commonplace.

The most seemingly harmless habitudes, those things we take for granted within ourselves and which, to us, are the very substance of life itself, the calm center from which we gaze upon and react to our world, are the things to look for, and we can assure ourselves with just a little self-study that these are indeed the most deadly of all our enemies; they indicate an area where we unconsciously deceive ourselves, legitimize machine habits, and blur our scale of realization.

This is generally the exact point in the labyrinth where we inevitably downscale into the human sector, the vortex which most powerfully draws us back into the zone of pain from which we have not yet been able to escape, and from which the only real escape is to alter our whole morphology of being.

Attention is the key for effective voyaging in the labyrinth, for our own work and also for the Work itself, because attention is the primary tool of the essential self.

When we exert the will of attention, placing it upon something without imposing itself upon it, without contaminating the object of attention with our personal and subjective interpretations, without clouding it with unknowing, with superficial animal significance which changes our perception and understanding of its nature, only then can we allow it to be, and in this way we can also be.

Our perceptions are so impregnated with human primate significances that we can count on them to be wrong, wrong in the hallucinatory sense; we cannot see what is there, only what we expect to be there. Our sensations, however, if we have trained ourselves in higher and more intuitive, more inquisitive, penetrative and encompassing, domain-devouring sensing skills utilizing our presence as the sensing apparatus and not the machine's sensations, can be depended upon, especially in the macrodimensional state, to reveal the truth behind the visual hallucination.

We must learn to experience things as they are, not as the mind wishes them to be. This is not the easiest attitude to achieve; after all, it requires of us that we retrain our whole perceptual apparatus and information processing system, and that we throw out everything we want to believe, the tinted glasses that make the Emerald City green.

As long as the headbrain is the source of awareness and attention, representing to ourselves and to others our totality of being, we will continue to produce these headbrain hallucinations, and we are destined to follow the machine down into identification; our attention will continue to explode into infinitesimal fragments at every little distracting factor; we will continue to find ourselves caught up in the trivial social-emotional significance of events as we play out our part in the daytime soap opera of primate life.

If we can find the attention of the essential self, and then train it, give it the skills necessary for life in the labyrinth, we can do anything; we literally can move mountains.

Until it is understood that it is not a question of *being here now*, but *being here more*, we won't be able to do anything to improve our situation.

We will eventually come to the realization that what we are looking at is what we are, no matter how we feel, no matter how we think of ourselves at the moment, we cannot be other than what we are looking at. We will see that our self-image is a convenience to assume a viewpoint, but we are actually looking at what we are. We are not looking at something other than ourselves.

We are alone, yet not alone, and must someday come to accept our endless fate as a single being existing alone forever, surrounded by flashing, distracting hallucinations, the dancing vision which springs from the pain of eternity.

The *Shabbas* is considered a day of rest; in fact, the ancients knew that it was to be a day of work, the day we give to the Absolute; six days a week we work to feed our faces, to insure our basic survival, but on the seventh day we give over our time, our energy and our attention totally to the service of the Absolute. Yet if we knew how, we could work every day.

We know that this would be the right course, but we have no idea how we should go about it.

Two things come immediately to mind; first, that inevitably, no matter what we do, we will experience a certain amount of biological involvement and environmental distraction.

We know that no matter where we are, no matter where we go, even into a school community in which we traverse the distance, make the passage from our present position in which we prepare ourselves for the Work to actually doing the Work, and we should remember that we will work in the Work long before we are actually *in* the Work, we will do essentially the same things that we did before; we are not free from our primate hungers just because we seem to be in a different location, even a community of work.

Even the fact that we are surrounded by more reminding factors in a work community offers little assurance; eventually everything—even work itself—blends into the general humdrum of background noise if our attention is still rooted in the machine.

In order to work seriously we must clear away the obstructions to work—and there are obstacles. Without obstacles, we would gain nothing from being in the school, there would be no profit. There are actually more obstacles to work in the school than there are in ordinary life, which makes the work even more valuable. Obstacles, if they are the right sort of obstacles, make us tougher and more able, if we are also at the same time able to keep a healthy, balanced perspective.

We want exercises for attention
But we don't want to use attention
In our lives.

E.J. GOLD, *LE DEJEUNER,* ACRYLIC ON CANVAS, 32'' x 40'', 1986.

AUTHOR'S AFTERWORD

JUST A WEE LITTLE MACRODIMENSIONAL
MATTER YET TO BE CLEARED UP

The use of the words "morphology" and "topology" present difficulties which perhaps could use further clarification.

A change in morphology very often is concurrent with a change in topology.

The word "morphology" is usually interpreted to mean shape, while topology is completely independent of shape. Two morphologically similar figures might possess the same topology, but we cannot say that if two figures have the same topology they necessarily have the same morphology.

The concept of morphology allows us to understand more clearly the idea of absorption of topological domains and our assumption by expansion of macroforms within macrotopologies.

We can expand into morphological configurations which coincide to any macrotopology; shapeshifting is the exact method we use to expand from the human biological morphology into a macromorphic configuration. When the higher is like the lower, and the lower is like the higher, then the dimensional morphologies coincide, and we make the two one; we transfer automatically into the corresponding macrodimensional configuration.

Any number of different morphologies should be able to enter the same topological domain or group of domains; there's no reason why an infinite number of morphologies could not occupy any topological configuration, but not any given morphological configuration.

Miniatures can function as shapeshifting connectors even though they may be very different in scale not only from the macro, but also different in scale in relation to the human biological machine... Scale is irrelevant in the practice of macromorphological shapeshifting.

In ordinary geometry there are two notions, the notion of congruence and the notion of similarity. In this case, we are developing the science of similarity, not congruence. Congruence means the same shape and size. Similarity means the same shape but not necessarily the same size, because size and scale are irrelevant to morphology.

We use congruence in a topological or geometric context to determine connected boundary domains where one boundary is congruent. They're not side by side, coincidental or superimposed; they're congruent, which means that the boundary is the same for both—a shared boundary in the sense that we use the same points on the boundary to define both domains, and that the same boundary is included in the consideration of each domain, as in the standard geography question, "which two provinces are separated by the B.C.-Alberta border?" (answer: Northwest Territories and Saskatchewan).

Through the use of infinitesimals and linear algebra, we can describe an enormous number of topological configurations of any given model... cut the pie in a variety of ways, as in "what is the capitol of Canada?" (answer: about seventy cents American).

We can extend—or perhaps even occasionally contract—our morphology until it coincides with the topology of the chamber, irrespective of scale; because scale is not a consideration, we can use a miniature for this purpose.

We could set up an experimental and experiential morphological extension, working outward from the human biological machine throughout which we have already extended our attention and presence to its outermost bounds, advancing our attention, presence and even sensing through a given morphology even if constructed in miniature.

We might find it more difficult to assume specific macromorphologies, given that we're extending ourselves outward from the platform of human primate, with which we are powerfully identified; after all, our whole sense of identity is caught up in the human form, and our sense of commitment to it is very strong. Were we to suddenly alter this form into a new and strange morphology, the sense of identity might not stand the strain, leaving us in a fear-reaction, fighting against ego-threat—not the kind you get from your girlfriend or boyfriend becoming aggressive, but the kind which really portends an end to identity as we presently understand ourselves to be and from which we act, think, and to which we turn for comfort and a sense of continuity.

Extending the boundaries of our morphological identity in a domain-devouring tour through external objects we find that we have full presence in the new morphology, including sensing, mood, perception and memory. We are now more than just a biological machine and an object, however; we are now something entirely different, which just coincidentally happens to resemble the two lumped together.

Let us suppose that the object into which we experimentally extend our morphology is a chair; not just any chair—but a Biedermeier . . . but we don't happen to have one of those on hand, and for one reason or another, can't get hold of or manufacture one—it's the weekend and there isn't a cabinet shop open—so we make a miniature model, and placing a fingertip on the seat of the model chair, we extend beyond our present human biological morphology well into the chair, obtaining as a result the morphological construct of human biological machine plus chair; using this method, we can produce a variety of morphological configurations which we can modify topologically just by altering the posture of one of the figures; crossing the legs and arms of the biological machine part of the new morphology, or eating a donut but leaving the hole.

Morphology is contained within the figure, but topology is a mathematical model imposed upon it; topology is not intrinsic to the figure; we superimpose topology on it atom-to-atom; the key idea in topology is the idea of neighborhood, two things being not continuous, but close to each other; it all depends upon what topology we're putting onto the physical situation.

If we slice a donut, we've probably got a good reason; we might want to produce two topological sections which used to be in the same neighborhood, or we're in a donut shop and we're sharing.

From one topological point of view, there's no longer a neighborhood that encompasses them both, and the two parts have become disconnected.

But from another topological point of view, the neighborhood can be viewed as still existing, even though not perceptually connected; it all depends on how we define "neighborhood", whether we go to the first or second topological definition, or still a third, Rogerian definition:

won't   you   please,   won't you please,

please won't you be   my   neigh-bor?

In the second of the three given morphological-topological models, neighborhoods would be created by domain connectivity between the spinal portion of the human biological machine and the front section of the back of the chair. Crossing and locking the legs would from this consideration be a much more radical topological alteration with much more far-reaching social and psycho-sexual implications than facing away from the chair.

Topology should be seen as an intrusive imposed mechanism, a way of looking at something. We cannot say that the thing itself has mathematics, we can only imply from outside the notion of measure and proportion; with mathematics, even a pyramid—meaningless in the objective sense—can be made to represent anything, even distant star-systems and cosmic laws, as long as we don't mind switching mathematics in midstream.

Number variances are determined by what measure we impose; in the case of macrodimensional morphological extension, we must impose topology on the object or space, in order to define its total connectivity, within which we can find boundaried morphologies toward which we may extend to gain entrance into one or another topological domain.

We should be aware of the three branches of mathematics in the abstract; algebra, topology and analysis, each of which is a different way of looking at fundamentally the same general characteristics. For instance, in algebra and in topology, we don't study urine samples, but in certain types of analysis, we definitely would.

We don't really need topology and morphology to explain morphological extension; just a few years ago, we might have utilized animal and plant forms in our shaman-to-shaman shop-talk ... we would speak of going coyote, going buffalo, or if we were voyaging in the vegetable kingdom, and very rattled, of going completely out of our gourd.

As a matter of fact, there are a number of books on shamanism which do suggest that one assume the coyote or the serpent eating its tail, or the roadrunner, or the rabbit, the baldheaded hunter, the black duck or the cwazy wabbit, but this is an unworkable formulation for our present culture;

of course, for all we know, it may have been just as unworkable fifty-thousand years ago; we can't be entirely sure how well these ideas were abused by those who went before us.

We need none of these ancient stylizations, however; we could just as easily designate the morphological constructs as in the Periodic Table of Angels.

Let's just say that what we're trying to do is eliminate restrictions and occlusions on our sense of identity, expanding our sensations, feelings and perceptions through a variety of morphological assumptives, not all of which are entirely rational.

Varying morphologies can be extended into the same topological configuration; moving invocants around in a circle might change the morphology somewhat, but the topological configuration remains the same.

The skills of morphological extension—shapeshifting—are acquired through morphological corresponding, adaptation, expansion, or similarity, determined by the objective topological configuration and found or artificially defined but stable morphological sub-sets within the target chamber.

The overall configuration of the chamber can be considered to be the topology of the chamber, within which we may be able to define corresponding morphologies which can give us presence in the chamber; as we are presently, we consider ourselves a more or less autonomous, individual, singular, separate, unique and inviolable form in the human; for our voyaging to be effective, we must find the psycho-emotional freedom to allow the morphos to change.

If macrodimensional voyaging calls for expansion of morphology, we could easily expect that downward voyaging will call for morphological contraction; as voyagers we will find it necessary to accommodate morphologically and psycho-emotionally, shapeshifting our way across the dimensions in accordance with the rapidly changing topological demands of the voyage.

The human morphology does not offer presence in a large number of macrodimensional chambers; the problem for us is that we're so strongly identified with the human morphos that, although we might be able to bring ourselves to add or subtract a few details, we're basically stuck with the same morphological configuration that we were born with.

We find it difficult indeed to break the bounds of that familiar electrical field which we see and feel as a comfortable enclosure, encapsulating and defining our identity-domain; weird distortions obtain in different dimensions, weird at least from the human primate point of view. We must, as voyagers, change this point of view until we can accept ourselves in widely varying format without losing the sense of identity which is independent of shape and definition of form.

It is this sense of identity—the kind we can't lose in a shapewreck and which remains standing in the face of death when everything else is burned away, dissolving in the unforgiving conflagration, and with the sense of identity, a strong and clearly delineated memory and understanding—which we develop through the technology of macromorphology.

Part of shamanism and voyaging in general is this life-extending shapeshifting, extending the morphology, and therefore the potential presence, in a much wider range throughout the spectrum of existence.

Our sense of identity originates in and is connected to the human biological machine; it gives us a very specific and seemingly safe idea of ourselves, which to the uneducated and uninitiated appears very stable and unvarying; if the morphology had been different, our sense of identity would have been differently developed, and we wouldn't be in the shape we're in now.

As we begin to work with morphological extension, our morphology ceases to be limited by the form of the human biological machine. We begin to realize that we are able to allow ourselves to be a connected part in a much larger unit, with a very different sense of identity and an extended, impersonal will, no longer just a primate; our total identity is much more complex, more cosmologically cosmopolitan.

If we can allow ourselves to extend our morphology even a little outside the primate domain, we've already extended our lives, because we now begin to exist in domains in which the human biological machine doesn't exist, but our new morphology does; this is true life extension, far beyond the biological meaning of the phrase.

Whole body attention is a necessity for morphological extension; we expand outward from the platform of a basic occupation of the machine with the fullest possible attention and presence; in extension, we must match the intensity of attention and presence of the domain into which we extend, the matching impedances producing an automatic homogeneous reconciliation of the forces of presence and attention in the blending of the two formerly irreconcilable domains.

APPENDICES

APPENDIX 1

Macrodimensions: A Mathematical Model

When we begin studying the labyrinth, we are confronted with new ideas of the world which are radically different from those we acquire in our ordinary efforts to survive in the organic world. We hear that in addition to our own familiar dimension, there is a hierarchy of "macrodimensions", which exist in exactly the same place and have exactly the same appearance as our own dimension, yet are qualitatively different. This concept may even be incomprehensible at first, yet is necessary for an understanding of the labyrinth.

This is a situation very familiar to the modern theoretical physicist. He learns that Einstein's theories of relativity require that what we ordinarily call "time" be viewed as a fourth spatial dimension. Yet at the outset of his scientific training, his ordinary spatio-temporal concepts cannot accommodate a fourth spatial dimension, let alone the treatment of time as spatial in nature.

The physicist acquires an intuition of these ideas by developing an understanding of certain abstract mathematical theories. Once he learns the theory of *linear algebras,* he can understand ordinary volume as a *vector space spanned by three orthogonal basis vectors,* which by convention he calls X, Y and Z. It is then trivial to generalize this model to any number of dimensions, to deduce the properties of n-dimensional spaces by analogy to his understanding of 3-space, and to verify his analogies through mathematical proof, should that be necessary.

Perhaps a mathematical theory of macrodimensions will help us understand, or at least tolerate, these new ideas. Let us begin by pointing out that the existence of one universe within a larger universe which has the same internal structure (at least when viewed from the smaller universe) is a common idea in modern abstract mathematics. A case in point is the development in the past few decades of *non-standard analysis.*

The *real numbers* are the positive and negative integers, rationals (fractions) and irrationals, which may be understood intuitively as representing all possible points on a line which extends indefinitely in each direction, with a reference point called "0" and a unit length called "1":

$$\langle \text{---.---.---.---.---.---.---.---.---.---.---.---} \rangle$$
$$\ldots \quad -4 \quad -3 \quad -2 \quad -1 \quad 0 \quad 1 \quad 2 \quad 3 \quad 4 \quad \ldots$$

In order to study a mathematical structure such as the reals (also called the *continuum*), the formal mathematician selects a minimal *vocabulary* of concepts (in this case the relations $+$, x and $>$) and attempts to construct a minimal set of statements, called a *theory,* from which other properties of the structure can be deduced using only the rules of inference of the first order predicate calculus.

From the theory of the reals, many properties can be deduced. For example, the continuum has the topological properties of *density,* i.e., between every two points there is at least one other point (and therefore an infinite number of points) and *closure,* i.e., every convergent series of points has a limit point.

However, it is possible for structurally different (non-isomorphic) models to satisfy the same theory; in fact, for any structure as complex as the reals, structurally different models necessarily satisfy the same theory. The number line described above is called the *standard model* of the reals and, intuitively speaking, consists of the numbers we ordinarily represent in decimal notation as a series of digits, which may be terminating or infinitely repeating, or may possess no repeating pattern.

However, through a simple application of the completeness theorem, we can add to the standard model a new number, the *infinitesimal* δ, which is a positive number less than any integral fraction, i.e., which satisfies the statements:

$$\delta > 0, \quad \delta < 1, \quad \delta < \tfrac{1}{2}, \quad \delta < \tfrac{1}{3}, \quad \delta < \tfrac{1}{4} \ \ldots$$

As a result, each real r_0 in the standard model is replaced with an entire continuum of numbers $r_0 + r_1\delta$, where r_1 is another standard real:

In fact, this process of replacing each point with an entire continuum is repeated of necessity an infinite number of times, since each point $r_0 + r_1\delta$ is surrounded by a yet smaller continuum of real multiples of the second order infinitesimal δ^2, which are surrounded by real multiples of δ^3, etc. Moreover, the entire standard continuum is itself surrounded by another continuum consisting of real multiples of the "infinite" number δ^{-1}, etc. Once we add δ to the structure, we are forced to add all bidirectional polynomials of the form:

$$\ldots r_{-n}\delta^{-n} + \ldots + r_{-2}\delta^{-2} + r_{-1}\delta^{-1} + r_0 + r_1\delta + r_2\delta^2 + \ldots + r_n\delta^n + \ldots$$

The new model is definitely different from the standard model. There is no *isomorphism* (structure-preserving one-to-one mapping) between the two models, but the new model contains the standard model as a substructure. In this sense (not in the sense of cardinality), we can say that it contains "more points", that it is a richer model. It is "the same, only more so", a macrodimensional model of the reals.

Another interesting fact about these two models may be analogous to the nature of macrodimensions: although the two models have different internal structures, that difference is impossible to describe with the linguistic tools available within the models. Any statement we can formulate using the vocabulary of the reals, such as the properties of density and closure, if true in the standard model, can also be true in a non-standard model.

Thus we have an interesting mathematical example of a universe (model) existing within a larger universe (an extension of that model), having the same internal structure but greater richness (a non-isomorphic extension of the original structure).

Since we now know this is possible in principle, we want to consider what the actual details of our model of macrodimensionality should be. Any mathematical model is necessarily an abstraction, a simplification of reality by the isolation of specific aspects which can be represented in precise formal language. Thus we need to find one or more central aspects of macrodimensionality which will comprise the vocabulary of our model.

Let us consider some characteristics of attention, viewed from an information-theoretic framework. Ordinary attention is definitely limited, though not necessarily fixed, in quantity. When we perform the simple psychological experiment of concentrating our attention on a small object, we discover that as the scope of our attention decreases, the amount of detail perceived increases. The greater amount of detail corresponds to a greater information density, just as greater clarity on a computer-graphics monitor requires a higher pixel density.

The total quantity of information processed I, measured in bits or some other suitable measure, might be represented as the product of the angular area A encompassed by the visual attention and the information density D:

$$I = A \times D$$

The approximately-inverse relationship between the scope of visual attention and the information density perceived then suggests that the total information-processing capability of the ordinary attention is, if not exactly fixed, at least bounded.

Since the information density of the attention is not constant over the visual field, but is highest in the central focal area, diminishing rapidly toward the peripheral vision, a more accurate representation would require an integral expression:

$$I = \int D(A) \, dA$$

To further generalize, we are not speaking simply of visual attention, but at the very least, of all the information processing capability of the organic machine, from all the senses, of data deriving from both outside and inside the body. Thus the space we are integrating over is not the geometrical space of spherical angles, but a space of possible units of information which could be available to the attention.

In order to give this abstract expression, let us create a space P consisting of points p_0, p_1, etc., which we will call *unit perceptions,* each of which represents a unique unit of information which could be processed by the attention, so that P contains all possible perceptions. Let us further assume that we define a topology T over P, in which the open sets t_0, t_1, etc. represent neighborhoods of similar perceptions, and that it is possible to define a measure μ over the topology, where $\mu(t_n)$ represents the total amount of information contained in the open set t_n. A given distribution of the attention can then be represented by a statistical *clarity function* C over the points in P, where C(p) gives the fraction of the available information in a neighborhood of p which is actually being processed by the attention (so $0 \leq C(p) \leq 1$). The total information I processed by the attention is then:

$$I = \int_p C(p) \; d\mu$$

Each clarity function represents a unique distribution of the attention over the data potentially available to it, and thus a unique state of the attention in relationship to its environment. Now it is certainly the case that not all C are in fact possible for the ordinary attention. In the first place, there is some upper bound I_0 to the amount of information which can be processed by the ordinary attention (allowing for the wide variance between individuals, and for a given individual, between states), so if C_0 represents an arbitrary clarity function of the ordinary attention,

$$\int_p C_0(p) \; d\mu \; < \; I_0$$

Even among functions C which satisfy this bound, many are not possible for the ordinary attention because they represent a distribution of attention which it cannot attain. We can characterize the dimensionality of our experience by the set of possible states of attention-distribution which are available to it, so in general we will define a *dimension* D_α as a set of clarity functions C_α.

In order to study the properties of a hierarchy of dimensions, we need to define a relation $\gg$ between dimensions, where $D_\beta \gg D_\alpha$ is read "D_β *is macro relative to* D_α". This is not a subset relationship, because in general, if C_α is a clarity function in D_α, we do not necessarily expect to find the same clarity function in the macro dimension D_β, but instead a function C_β which has at least the clarity of C_α at all p, if not more. To formalize this, we define C_β to *encompass* C_α, written $C_\beta > C_\alpha$, by:

$$C_\beta > C_\alpha \equiv (\forall p)\, (C_\beta\,(p) \geq C_\alpha\,(p)\,)$$

Then we can define D_β to be macro to D_α by:

$$D_\beta \gg D_\alpha \equiv (\forall C_\alpha)\, (\ C_\alpha \epsilon D_\alpha \rightarrow (\exists C_\beta)\, (C_\beta \epsilon D_\beta\ \&\ C_\beta > C_\alpha)\,)$$

One conclusion which can be drawn from these definitions is that, at least mathematically speaking, there is a least-macro dimension and a most-macro dimension. We can define the *total obscurity function* C_{min} for which $C_{min}\,(p) = 0$ for all p. All C encompass C_{min}, so the dimension D_{min}, which contains only C_{min}, is lower than all other dimensions. Conversely, we can define the *total clarity function* C_{max} for which $C_{max}(p) = 1$ at all points p (meaning that 100% of the data from each possible perception is being processed). C_{max} is easily seen to encompass all C. Therefore a dimension D_{max} which contains C_{max} is higher than any other dimension.

All other dimensions lie between D_{min} and D_{max}, including the ordinary organic dimension, represented as D_0. Since it is mathematically possible for two dimensions D_α and D_β to be *incomparable*, meaning that neither $D_\alpha \gg D_\beta$ nor $D_\beta \gg D_\alpha$, the structure of dimensions is a *partial ordering*, with multiple paths from D_{min} to D_{max}:

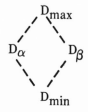

Thus we have created the beginnings of a simple formal language in which many ideas of macrodimensionality can be expressed. Many possibilities are now evident for expanding on these ideas mathematically in order to express more detailed information about dimensionality. For example, certain perceptual shifts in the macrodimensional experience, such as the perception of greater distance between objects and the sensation of greater resistance to movement, can be understood and expressed in information-theoretic terms.

This mathematical model is also useful in refining the questions for empirical study, as our aim is not simply to study the mathematical properties of an arbitrary structure, but to improve our understanding of the real world through an accurate model. We need to ask questions such as: what does P contain? (i.e., what types of data are potentially available to the attention?); what restrictions need to be added to the definition of the clarity functions C? (i.e., in what possible ways can the attention be distributed); and, what restrictions need to be added to the definition of the dimensions D? (i.e., what dimensions other than D_0 actually exist, if any?).

APPENDIX 2

Macrodimensions:
A Physical Perspective

This paper is a preliminary sketch showing how some of the ideas of macrodimensional voyaging might be expressed using the terminology of modern physics, resulting from a brain-storming session at the Institute. Many ideas are quickly suggested without detailed definition, opening possibilities for a much more extensive and complete development along physical lines.

As defined in Appendix 1, the total clarity function C_{max} equals 1 at all points p, meaning that the total available information is being processed by the attention. The integral of C_{max} over P then represents the total information processed in the highest macrodimension:

$$A_{tot} = \int C_{max}(p) \, d\mu$$

For further discussion, however, it would be more convenient if we normalized the attention integral so that its maximum value was 1, giving a formulation easier for the average graduate level physicist to understand, but not spell or punctuate. Once normalized, an integral of 1 represents total clarity, an integral of 0 represents total occlusion, and other values represent the portion of the available information being processed. We can do this by integrating with respect to $d\mu / A_{tot}$ instead of $d\mu$. Then:

$$0 \leq \int C(p) \ d\mu / A_{tot} \leq 1$$

Let us define occlusion factor O as the complement of the above integral, i.e.:

$$O(C) = 1 - \int C(p) \ d\mu / A_{tot}$$

Thus the highest dimension has an occlusion of 0 and the lowest dimension has an occlusion of 1, or total occlusion.

Now let us assume that occlusion is quantized. From a physical point of view this is plausible, since one would be hard pressed to find any phenomenon which is not quantized. To make this specific, let us assume that there is a finite, though very large, number N of discrete points p in our informational topology. Let us assume also that at each point p, the clarity functions C can assume M+1 discrete values from 0 to 1 in multiples of 1/M. From these assumptions, we can deduce that the occlusion O can take on MxN+1 discrete values from 0 to 1, in multiples of o $=$ 1/m x 1/N, where o is the quanta of occlusion.

Let us define two clarity functions which have the same integrated occlusion to be isothermic. We can now compute the number of isothermic clarity functions for a given occlusion factor using combinatorial techniques.

Beginning at the top of the tree, there is only one clarity function which will yield an occlusion of 0, $C_{max}(p)$, since C(p) must equal 1 for all p. There are N possible clarity functions with an occlusion of 1o, since a clarity function will possess this occlusion only if C(p)=1 for all p except for one point p' where C(p') $=$ 1 - 1/M. Continuing this reasoning using combinatorial techniques, we can compute that there are N(N+1)/2 clarity functions with occlusion 2o,

$N(N+1)(N+2)/6$ clarity functions with occlusion 3o, etc. Thus the number of clarity functions rises very rapidly with the value of O.

If we consider the bottom of the tree — absolute occlusion — we see that here again only one clarity function has an occlusion factor of 1, that N clarity functions have occlusion 1-o, $N(N+1)/2$ clarity functions have occlusion 1-2o, etc.

To generalize our notation, we will represent a clarity function $C(p)$ with an integrated occlusion of O' as $Co'(p)$. The total number of clarity functions with integrated occlusion O' can be notated as $N(O')$. We can deduce that $N(O')$ is minimum at $O=0$ and $O=1$, and increases monotonically from these end-points to a maximum value at $O'=.5$, around which $N(O')$ is symmetric. In fact, for large M and N, the function $N(O')$ becomes a Poisson distribution — the classic bell curve.

We now wish to analyze transitions of the voyager from one clarity function state to another. We will define a state change between two clarity functions of the same occlusion factor to be an isothermal or lateral transition, and a state change between clarity functions of differing occlusion a macrodimensional or vertical transition.

Let us first consider isothermal transitions, since these are presumably the type we make most often. At a given occlusion O', there are $N^2(O')$ possible transition pairs. We will call this figure the raw connectivity at O'.

We can view these clarity function transitions as forming a network, with the individual clarity functions as nodes, and the transitions as paths between these nodes. The raw connectivity indicates an upper bound for the density of connectivity of a given isothermal plane. By assigning a probability weight to each path, however, the density of connectivity will be reduced by trimming the improbable transitions. It is the mapping of this macrodimensional network and the plotting of transitions within its framework that shall serve as the focus for the remainder of this treatise.

As a simple physical analogy, consider the quantum mechanics of the hydrogen atom. In this case, there is a well-defined process for calculating the probability of an electron making a transition from one state to another. Using the resulting equations, the physicist can determine methods for the enhancement and selection of particular transitions, by exploring the contributing factors in the formula.

We propose to establish a corresponding expression for the probability of clarity function state transitions. We wish to obtain at least a partial expansion of the function $\text{Prob}(C_a, C_b)$, the probability of a clarity function state transition from C_a to C_b. Using our knowledge or assumptions concerning clarity function state transitions, we will express some of the factors which effect the probability of state transitions in mathematical form, so we can determine means of increasing the probability of macro-dimensional transitions.

By analogy with physical examples, one factor which contributes to $P(C_a, C_b)$ might be the overlap integral of the two clarity functions:

$$\text{Prob}(C_a, C_b) = Q(\ ) \ \text{Overlap} \ (C_a, C_b)$$

where:

$$\text{Overlap} \ (C_a, C_b) = \int K(p) \ C_a(p) \ C_b(p) \ d\mu$$

and $Q(\ )$ is an expression containing the remaining, as yet undetermined, terms of the formula. We can loosely define the overlap integral to be a measure of the similarity of the two clarity functions. Thus our expression tells us that the more similar two clarity functions, the higher the probability of transition.

This overlap integral suggests the need to consider the hysteresis or latent field memory of the voyager, since the higher the voyager's hysteresis, the greater the contribution of the overlap integral. In other words, the more the voyager requires things to be the same, the lower the probability of transition into non-similar clarity functions. In the case of a voyager with high hysteresis, this effect will tend to lock the voyager into a series of repeating and quite similar clarity

A2-4

functions. The substitution of one hysteresis for another does not alter this situation, only the domain of occupancy.

The overlap integral also suggests the need to consider interference effects. If the voyager tends to oscillate between many isothermic clarity functions because of the effect of non-considered forces, a phenomenon which corresponds to Brownian movement, this will tend to interfere with and cancel the probability for vertical transitions. In other words, "If you don't sit still, how can you expect to catch a lift?" This effect of interference is most noticeable in the lower dimensions where the Brownian dance dramatically outweighs the all-but-zero probability of macrodimensional transitions.

Another factor which likely contributes to Prob (C_a, C_b) is some function of the values of the occlusion factors of the two clarity functions:

$$\text{Prob } (C_a, C_b) = Q'\,(\ )\ \text{Overlap } (C_a, C_b)\ F(O_a, O_b)$$

Certainly, the greater the difference between the two occlusion factors, the lower we expect the state change probability to be.

Moreover, we propose on the basis of empirical data that if O_a is close to zero, $F(O_a, O_b)$ gives a higher weight to macrodimensional transitions than to isothermal transitions, and that if O_a is large compared to zero, isothermal transitions are heavily favored.

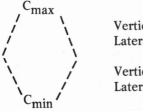

Vertical transitions $\sim$ 1
Lateral transitions $\sim$ 0

Vertical transitions $\sim$ 0
Lateral transitions $\sim$ 1

A2-5

In the upper regions of the macrodimensional network, lateral transfers are all but impossible and macrodimensional transitions predominate in probability. We could say that, for all practical purposes, a voyager in these regions has nowhere to go that is any different than where he is except to someplace that is the same only a little more or less so. In the lower regions of the macrodimensional network where lateral transitions dominate in probability, the Brownian dance reduces the probability of macrodimensional transitions from their already all-but-zero probability to something so close to zero that "Why shouldn't we call it zero anyway?"

A third factor which might influence the probability of particular state transitions is the length of time a given state has been occupied. If the voyager maintains a state C_a for a longer period of time, not only is the effect of Brownian dance limited, but the probability of vertical transitions is actually increased. We can express this effect through the addition of a time-averaging function T to our function Prob (C_a, C_b):

$$\text{Prob}(C_a, C_b) = Q''() \text{ Overlap}(C_a, C_b) \; F(O_a, O_b) \; T(t, C_a, C_b)$$

where t is the time of uninterrupted occupancy of clarity function C_a.

One result of the structure of the function T might be called the occlusion of opportunity, which introduces the effects of temporal lumpiness in an otherwise homogeneous field of opportunity for macrodimensional transitions. In other words, what is possible one moment may not be as possible the next moment. The occlusion of opportunity is inversely proportional to motivation, caring and directed attention.

Let us review the current expression for $\text{Prob}(C_a, C_b)$ and direct our attention to the question of what methods are available to increase the probability of vertical transitions.

1) The hysteresis and other field predisposition effects of the voyager can be modified, thereby shifting domains of available clarity functions.

2) The coupling between the voyager and non-considered forces can be reduced, diminishing the Brownian motion effect on the state of the voyager, thereby increasing the amount of uninterrupted time spent in a single clarity function and the probability of vertical transitions.

3) Motivation, caring and directed attention can be increased, thereby decreasing the negative effects of occlusion of opportunity.

With the possible exception of the occlusion of opportunity modifier, the factors placed under consideration so far have been localized field effects, components of the macrodimensional network itself. With only these factors operant, the resulting physics will be stochastic and follow the basic laws of thermodynamics. In this case, it would be only through the intercession of Maxwell's Demons that we would be able to work.

However, by incorporating presence effects into the expression for $\text{Prob}(C_a, C_b)$, we set the stage for consideration of non-stochastic effects, since we are now considering modifications of transition probabilities through the voyager's internal state.

The effect of presence on the probability of transition might be expressed as follows:

$$\text{Prob}(C_a, C_b) =$$

$$Q'''(\ ) \ \text{Overlap}(C_a, C_b) \ F(O_a, O_b) \ T(t, C_a, C_b) \ \text{Overlap}(E, C_b)$$

where:

$$\text{Overlap}(E, C_b) = \int E(p) \ C_b(p) \ d\mu$$

and $E(p)$ is a function describing the distribution of the presence of the voyager, which we will call the morphology of presence. As a result of this new overlap integral, when the morphology of presence corresponds to the morphology of attention (the clarity function) of the target state, the probability of transition is increased by an expressible quantitative factor. The tendency to inhabit particular sections of the macrodimensional network can be explained by the habitual tendency of presence to hold certain morphologies which restrict it to a range of corresponding clarity functions.

Initially we can assume that the voyager is an occupant in some clarity function with a morphology of attention given by $C_a(p)$. The morphology of presence is bounded by the morphology of attention:

$$E(p) \leqslant C_a(p) \text{ for all } p$$

Almost without exception, the presence is bounded by a shape and size that is much less than the shape and size of attention. In particular, the voyager's presence will typically be limited by the confines of his human biological machine, but his attention may encompass many objects outside the machine.

However, the voyager can use this factor to force macrodimensional transitions by expanding the morphology of his presence to the limit of the morphology of attention. This greatly increases the probability of a macrodimensional transition to a clarity function with a morphology of attention that will contain the expanded morphology of presence.

Hysteresis or latent field memory effects will inhibit the free form expansion of the morphology of presence. This will effectively constrain the set of available clarity function transitions to a band of "acceptable" clarity functions. It is here we may have a clue to the nature of the Heart of the Labyrinth. Perhaps the Heart of the Labyrinth is not a specific clarity function or domain in the macrodimensional network, but a condition of undistorted presence lacking hysteresis or latent field memory, a condition in which the presence is not prejudicial to any particular clarity function and does not preclude any given clarity function.

INDEX

Letter to the Reader:

The intention of this book is not to provide final answers to all the questions which face a voyager cast adrift in the macrodimensions; no book can have such a pretense. It can, however, stimulate and nourish the questioning process in which real questions are always followed by still further questions.

A third book in this series published under the title *The Practical Guide to the Labyrinth* will provide another series of answers to questions which will inevitably develop from this material. Those of you who wish to work with this information will find it most valuable.

If, on the other hand, you feel an urgency to your questions and are prepared to work in a serious way, direct contact is perhaps the solution for you. You are therefore invited to formulate your questions by writing, phoning or eventually, after following the designated procedures, presenting yourself in person through the following address:

The Labyrinth Desk
Gateways Books
P.O. Box 370
Nevada City, CA 95959

or call (916) 477-1116.